COUNCIL OF THE COUNTY OF ABERDEEN
EDUCATION COMMITTEE

A
SCHOOL HISTORY
OF ABERDEENSHIRE

BY

JIM BUCHAN, M.A., Ed.B.

Deputy Headmaster of Culter School and
Principal Teacher of English Subjects

22 UNION TERRACE,
ABERDEEN.

This book is dedicated
to the memory of Charles Murray, C.M.G., LL.D.,
whose expressed wish it was that the children
of Aberdeenshire should be taught the history
of their native county.

SCHOOL HISTORY OF ABERDEENSHIRE

FOREWORD

Following the publication in 1950 of the Scottish Education Department's Memorandum "The Primary School in Scotland," panels of Aberdeenshire teachers prepared schemes of work taking into account the recommendations contained in the memorandum, and these schemes were issued to schools in 1953. In the course of their discussions on the teaching of history, the panels agreed that the study of local history should be given an important place and suggested that a School History of Aberdeenshire should be produced which would be suitable for pupils in the senior stages of the primary school.

In 1957, the Trustees of the Charles Murray Memorial Fund, after consultation with the County Head Teachers' Association, decided to offer an award of £50 to the writer of such a History provided that it was approved by themselves and by the Education Committee.

The Education Committee agreed to accept responsibility for the publication of the book and, with the approval of the Trustees, asked Mr. Jim Buchan to undertake the writing of it. On completion, this book was submitted to the Trustees and gained their award for the author.

The book is suitable not only for senior primary pupils but for pupils in the first three years of secondary courses and teachers in both departments will no doubt find it useful. Certain chapters — for example, the last four — have been written with secondary pupils particularly in mind. Mr. Buchan has referred to many parts of the County in the course of his story, so that pupils will have the thrill of reading about their own locality and its part in the story of our country. Within the scope of a small book he has succeeded remarkably well in imparting a great deal of information in a simple and interesting way. I am confident that the book will be welcomed in the schools and will justify the time, thought, and skill which Mr. Buchan has devoted to its composition.

ALEX. L. YOUNG,
Director of Education.

County Buildings,
22 Union Terrace,
Aberdeen.
March, 1961.

ACKNOWLEDGMENTS

In the writing of this book, I have been helped by many people. I owe a deep debt of gratitude to the authors, too numerous to name, of the books which I consulted. I am also indebted to those headmasters and members of the teaching staff in Aberdeenshire who read all, or part, of the book in manuscript and made many helpful suggestions.

For permission to reproduce the illustrations in the book I wish to thank the following:—

Mr. G. A. Baxter, M.A., B.A., and Mr. I. M. Davidson, B.Sc., for Nos. 2, 3, 6, 7, 10, 11, and 13.

Mr. Edward Meldrum, D.A., A.R.I.B.A., for Nos. 4 and 9.

Mearns Publications, Ltd., for Nos. 5 and 12.

The Deeside Field Club for No. 1.

Mr. R. Philip for No. 14.

Mr. J. S. Milne for No. 8.

Finally, I wish to record my gratitude to Mr. J. G. Gordon, M.A., Depute Director of Education for Aberdeenshire, for the willing assistance he has given and the many useful suggestions he has offered at all stages of the work.

JIM BUCHAN.

CONTENTS

ILLUSTRATIONS AND MAPS

All above Illustrations and Maps between
pages 54 and 55

INDEX

A

Aberdeen, 1, 7, 9, 10, 12, 19, 20, 23, 26, 28, 29, 31, 32, 34, 35, 36, 37, 39, 40, 41, 42, 43, 44, 45, 46, 47, 48, 49, 50, 51, 52, 53, 54, 56, 58, 59, 61, 62, 63, 64, 72, 78, 79-85, 86, 87, 91, 93, 95, 98, 99, 100, 101, 102, 103, 104, 105, 106, 107, 108, 109, 110, 111, 112, 113, 114, 115, 116, 117.
Aberdeen, 1st Earl of, 110.
Aberdeen, 3rd Earl of, 110.
Aberdeen, 7th Earl of, 110.
Aberdeen-Angus Cattle, 91, 94.
Aberdeen Assembly, 45.
Aberdeen Doctors, 47.
Aberdeenshire Road Act, 100.
Aberdour, 18, 20.
Abergeldie Castle, 73.
Aboyne, 4, 9, 11, 14, 16, 17, 20, 23, 24, 28, 51, 57, 59, 63, 66, 70, 100, 101.
Aboyne, Earl of, 87.
Aboyne, Viscount, 48, 49.
Adamnan, St., 17, 18, 20.
Agriculture, Society of Improvers in the Knowledge of, 87.
Aikey Brae, 10, 31, 89.
Aikey Fair, 89, 95.
Alford 6, 9, 10, 12, 19, 20, 36, 53, 54, 66, 68, 70, 72, 73, 90, 100, 101, 102, 115.
Alford, Battle of, 53, 54.
Anderson, Sir Alexander, 107.
Anderson, Sir George, 107.
Anderson, William, 92.
Arbuthnot, Bailie Thomas, 59, 61.
Argyll, Marquis of, 50-52.
Arnage Castle, 73.
Asloun Castle, 73.
Auchindoir, 3, 9, 25, 33, 39, 72.
Auchterless, 17, 47, 52, 64, 72, 92.

B

Baillie, General, 53, 54.
Baird, Charles, 98.
Baldyquash (Fyvie), 21.
Balfluig Castle, 73.
Balgreen (King Edward), 10.
Balhaggardy, 35, 36.
Ballater, 11, 13, 17, 64, 101.
Balmoral, 71.
Balmedie, 1.
Balquhain, 10, 34, 35, 36, 37, 41, 92, 112.
Balquhain Castle, 41, 64.
Banchory, 1, 12, 15, 101, 107.
Barbour, John, 107.
Barclay, Andrew, 106.
Barmekin of Echt, 13.
Barmekin of Keig, 13.
Barra, 13, 30, 31.
Barra, Battle of, 30-32, 36.
Bass of Inverurie, 9, 21, 25, 26, 27.
Beaker People, 4, 8, 14.
Belhelvie, 6, 9, 11, 15, 19, 109, 115.
Bennachie, 13, 90, 91.
Bieldside, 7.
Birse, 5, 20, 38, 66, 70.
Black Arthur, 43.
Black Arthur's Well, 43.
Blackhills (Tyrie), 9.
Black Jock of Invererran, 59.
Bobbing John (Earl of Mar), 58-61.
Boddam, 3, 102.
Boece, Hector, 84.
"Bon-Accord", 31.
Bon-Accord, Abbot and Prior of, 83.
Bonnie Dundee, 57, 69.
Bonnie Prince Charlie, 62, 63, 66.
Bourtie, 10, 24, 36.
Boyndlie, 4, 115.
Braemar, 54, 59, 61, 90, 100, 101, 112.
Braemar Castle, 57, 72.
Brandsbutt Stone, 14.
Bridge of Dee, Battle of the, 49.
Bronze Age, 4-7, 8, 9, 10, 11, 12, 14, 19.

Broomend of Crichie, 5, 21.
Bruce, David, 32-35.
Bruce, Edward, 30, 31.
Bruce, Nigel, 29, 30.
Bruce, King Robert, 29-33, 35, 68.
Bruce, Robert, 28.
Brux, 36, 66.
Buchan, Countess of, 29.
Buchan, 1st Earl of, 25.
Buchan, 3rd Earl of, 28-32.
Buchan, A Small Society of Farmers in, 87.
Buchan, General Thomas, 57.
Buchanhaven, 61.
Buchan humlies, 88, 94.
Bucksburn, 91, 98.
Burgesses, 80-82.
Burghs, 26, 80-81.
Burnett, Alexander, 32.
Burnett, Thomas, 86.
Burton, John Hill, 116.
Butcher Cumberland, 64.

C

Cairnbrogie, 7, 94.
Cairnbulg, 28, 92, 102.
Cairnbulg Castle, 72, 73.
Cairnie, 61, 90, 93.
Cairns, 4, 6, 7, 10.
Canal, Aberdeenshire, 100, 101.
Caranoc, St., 20.
Caskieben, 36, 112.
Castle Fraser, 49, 51, 57, 61, 71, 94.
Castle Newe, 11, 12.
Catto of Cairncatto, 107.
Celts, 11, 12, 14, 26.
Cementarius, Richard, 79.
Chalmers, James, 108.
Chapel of Garioch, 10, 19, 21, 41, 113.
Chapel of Seggat, 64.
Charlie, Bonnie Prince, 62, 63, 66.
Cheyne, George, 108.
Circles, Standing Stone, 5, 6, 10.
Cists, Short, 4, 5, 9.
Clatt, 6, 12, 19, 20, 21, 38, 80, 100.
Clinterty, 9.
Clippers, 102.
Clochmaloo, 16.
Clova, 5, 16.
Cluny, 27, 47.
Cluny Castle, 54, 71.
Collynie, 10, 94.
Colm, St., 16, 18, 19, 20.
Colquhoney, 72.
Columba, St., 17, 18.
Comgall, St., 16.
Comyn, William, 25.
Congan, St., 17.
Corgarff, 16, 35, 64, 66, 89, 90, 100.
Corgarff Castle, 43, 53, 72.
Corrichie, 41, 54.
Corrichie, Battle of, 40-42.
Corse Castle, 73.
Coull, 11, 25, 61, 68, 101.
Crabstane, 43, 52.
Craft Guilds, 81-83.
Craig, John of the, 33, 69.
Craig Castle, 72.
Craigievar, 35, 49, 53, 71.
Craigston Castle, 117.
Crannogs, 11, 12.
Crathie, 17, 19, 60, 100.
Creighton, Dr. Charles, 108.
Crichie, 5, 21, 30.
Crimond, 44, 59, 84, 91, 109.
Cruden, 3, 5, 6, 10, 22, 23, 25, 32, 44, 110.
Cruden, Alexander, 108.
Cruickshank, Amos and Anthony, 94.
Culblean, Battle of, 33, 34.
Cullerlie, 5, 41, 91.
Culsalmond, 20, 21, 35.
Culter, 28, 101, 105.
Cumberland, Duke of, 64, 65.
Cumine, Charles, 63.
Cumine, George, 60, 63.
Cumine, Joseph, 86.

Chapter 1

IN EARLIEST TIMES

Our story of Aberdeenshire begins more than eight thousand years before Jesus was born. At that time, towards the end of the **Ice Age,** large glaciers moved across the County, changing the shape of the land and forming many of the hills and valleys which we see to-day. Gradually it grew warmer and, after many years, the ice-sheets melted. The climate became warmer still and the land was thickly covered with bushes and trees. In time, wild animals, especially reindeer, came north into the forests and hunters began to follow them. The weapons and tools which these early people used were made of horn, bone, wood or stone. Most of those which have been found are made of stone and so we call the time when they were first used the **Stone Age.** It is sometimes divided into three parts — the Old Stone Age, the Middle Stone Age, and the New Stone Age. Nothing has been found to show that there were people living in Aberdeenshire during the Old Stone Age. As far as we know, it was during the Middle Stone Age that the County was first inhabited.

THE MIDDLE STONE AGE

The Strandloopers.

These early inhabitants did not grow crops, nor had they any tame animals, such as sheep or cows, which they could kill for food. They were hunters who, dressed in animal skins, did not live in the same place all the time but moved about in search, not only of wild animals, but also of shellfish, nuts, berries, and roots to eat.

Some of these primitive folk are called **Strandloopers** because they came along the coast in their small boats, going from one sandy beach, or strand, to the next. They went only short distances at a time, keeping in sight of land as far as possible and, while on the beaches, they may have lived in small tents made from animal skins. Big midden heaps of shells and bones, as well as many pieces of flint, which were left by these early wanderers, have been found at Nigg, to the south of Aberdeen; on the coast near the village of Balmedie; and at the mouth of the River Ythan.

Pygmy Flints.

At about the same time as the strandloopers were living on the coast — possibly between 4000 B.C. and 3000 B.C. — other people were living, probably in shallow pits roofed with animal skins or turf, where Banchory now stands. On both banks of the River Dee, very small flint tools have been found. They are called Pygmy Flints because they are so small, many of them being only about a quarter of an inch long. It is not certain what they were used for but a few of them may have been fixed to a piece of wood to make a tool like a saw. Several of them look as though they could have been used for boring holes in animals' skins, which were to be made into clothes. Whatever the use of these Pygmy Flints, they do show that the North-east was inhabited during the Middle Stone Age.

THE NEW STONE AGE

The First Farmers

During the New Stone Age, many of the people stopped wandering about constantly in search of food and began to live in the same place most of the time. Although they still hunted, they did not eat only the flesh of the wild animals which they had killed. They learned how to tame sheep, cattle, goats, pigs, and horses, and so they could use some of them for food. They also learned how to cultivate the land but they could not grow enough to meet all their needs and still had to collect fruit, nuts, berries, and roots.

To make a small plot for growing wheat, they first had to clear away the bushes and trees. If these were too big to be cut with stone axes, the New Stone Age farmers burned a clearing. They had no matches but rubbed two sticks together on top of a pile of dry grass until it caught fire. At other times, they might strike two pieces of flint together until the sparks had set the grass on fire. When the flames died out, the ashes which were left helped to manure the ground.

The New Stone Age farmer did not have a plough with which to turn over the soil. He used a digging-stick. This was a strong piece of wood, usually about four feet long and pointed at one end, near which a stone was fastened to add weight to the stick. The digging-stick was lifted up and dropped so that the sharp point went into the earth. The digging was not deep with such a tool, but later on the collar-bone of an animal was fixed to a piece of wood and so a kind of spade was made. Sometimes, a kind of hoe, made of the antlers of a deer or of a stone tied to a wooden handle, was used to turn over the ground before the seeds were planted. Again the digging was not deep, being often little more than a scratch on the surface of the soil.

When the corn was ripe it was cut with a sickle made from a piece of bone or wood, with sharp flint flakes fastened to it. Once the outside husks had been removed from the ears, they were scattered on a smooth, flat stone. Then a round stone was rubbed backwards and forwards over them until they were squashed flat and made into meal. The stones which were used for grinding in this way are known as **Saddle Querns,** because the bottom stone soon became worn in the middle until it was shaped like a saddle. Small pieces of stone often became mixed with the meal and quickly wore down the teeth of the people who ate it, sometimes right to the gums.

Flint Knapping and Flint Smiddies

The only place in Aberdeenshire where there is a supply of flint is on a ridge eight miles long, running south-west from Peterhead and most of the tools and weapons used in the County during the New Stone Age were made from flint found in that part of Buchan. It is possible that people living in other parts of the North-east gave furs and skins to those living around Stirling Hill near Boddam, in exchange for the flint, which was usually carried inland and then made into tools and weapons by men using stone hammers and stone anvils. This is known as **Flint Knapping.**

One of the weapons most often used was the bow-and-arrow. Feathers were fixed to the shaft so that the arrow would fly straight. The arrow-heads were made from thin flakes of flint and many have been found in Aberdeenshire at such places as New Deer, Methlick, and Ellon. New Stone Age men also used flint knives, scrapers, and sickles, as well as needles and other articles made from fish-bone.

The flint tools were made in Flint Smiddies. These were usually on high-lying ground since the people in early times lived on the slopes of the hills because the low-lying parts were wet and marshy. In 1955, some children from Bridge of Don School found the site of a smiddy on the hill to the landward side of the school.

Instead of making all their axes from flint, with chipped, jagged edges, as Middle Stone Age men had done, the New Stone Age people discoverd how to make them by polishing pieces of hard stone. By rubbing the stone with a piece of wood, or another stone, they could make an axe which was smooth and had a sharp, straight edge. This new kind of axe lasted longer than a flint one and was not so easily blunted. A New Stone Age axe made of flint was found at New Deer, while polished stone axes have been found, among other places, at Kildrummy and Cruden.

Clothing

The people dressed in the skins and furs of animals. Using a flint knife, they cut off the skin and removed the fat from the inside of it with a flint scraper. This was done not only to clean the skin, but also to prevent it from hardening. After this, the skin was stretched out tightly between pegs in the ground and was rubbed in order to soften it. The threads or cords which were used for sewing the skins were made of strips of hide, animal hairs twisted together, or plaited human hair.

Pottery

An important invention of New Stone Age men was the mak-ing of clay bowls, which they used for storing food. The bowls had no handles and were round-bottomed. They were made from coils of clay which, having been placed one on top of the other, were pressed together and then smoothed. A design was often made on the bowl by pressing the soft clay with the thumb-nail, an ear of corn, or the end of a piece of stick or bone. The bowl was then baked in a fire to harden it. Pieces of this New Stone Age pottery have been found at four places in Aberdeenshire — East Finnercy in Dunecht, Knapperty Hillock in Buchan, Fernie-brae in the Garioch, and Craig in Auchindoir.

Long Cairns.

The first farmers believed that when a man died he went to another world where he would need the kind of tools he had used in this world. They therefore put such things as flint knives and arrow-heads into the grave of the dead man. The burial-places are known as Cairns. There are various types of these in the British Isles ranging from the very elaborate structure at Maes Howe in Orkney to the very simple examples, appearing to be nothing more than heaps of stones, which we may see at the farm of Longcairn, Kingswells and in Balnagowan Wood, Aboyne. Since the New Stone Age Cairns in Aberdeenshire are long-shaped, they are known as Long Cairns.

THE BEAKER PEOPLE

Towards the end of the New Stone Age, a new people began to settle in Scotland. Between 2000 B.C. and 1800 B.C., these incomers, who were fairly short and had very round heads and strong, square jaws, crossed the North Sea from Holland and the land round the mouth of the River Rhine. Many of them landed on the sandy beaches of Aberdeenshire. They then moved inland and settled all over the County, but mostly between the River Don and the River Ythan.

Short Cist Burials

Instead of burying their dead in groups, in cairns, as the New Stone Age people had done, the new settlers buried them individually in Short Cists. The sides of these shallow graves, which were usually about three feet eight inches long, consisted of big, flat stones. The earth at the bottom of the cist was smoothed and, in some cases, covered with sand or pebbles. The body was buried on its side, with the arms and legs bent, and the large, flat cap-stone was placed in position and covered with earth.

Many short cists have been discovered not far below the surface of the ground by farmers when ploughing. A clay vase, or beaker, is usually found in the cist and so the people who made them are known as the **Beaker People.** Like the Stone Age men, the Beaker People believed that when a man died he went to live in another world exactly like the one he had left. To help the dead man on his journey to this new world, food was put into the beaker in the short cist. Tools, weapons, or ornaments were also put into the grave so that the man could use them in his second life. Flint scrapers, flint knives, flint arrow-heads, bone needles, clay beads, and slate wrist-guards for bowmen have been found in short cists.

Short cists have been found at many places in the County, including South Ythsie in Tarves, Whitestone Farm in Skene, and Upper Boyndlie.

THE BRONZE AGE

From about 1700 B.C., the inhabitants of Aberdeenshire made some of their tools and weapons of bronze, and so we call this time the Bronze Age. During the Bronze Age, they also learned how to weave cloth from wool and flax, so that they no longer wore only animal skins.

Tools, Weapons, and Ornaments

Bronze is made by mixing two metals, tin and copper, which are not found in Aberdeenshire, and so the people had to trade for them. Tin was taken from Cornwall in the south of England and copper was brought from Ireland. This meant that bronze was very dear and many people continued to use flint and stone tools, so that some of the flint smiddies, which we mentioned earlier, were still in operation during the Bronze Age.

Once the tin and copper had been melted together, the hot mixture was poured into a stone shape, or mould, and so made into tools and weapons. Stone moulds which were used during the Bronze Age for making axe-heads and daggers were discovered on the Foudland Hill near Insch. Other Bronze Age moulds were found at Kintore. Many bronze weapons have been unearthed in Aberdeenshire; for example, axes at Tarland and Forest of Birse, swords at Daviot and Schivas, daggers at Clova and Towie, and shields at Auchmaleddie near New Deer. At Braes of Gight on the River Ythan, bronze pins, necklets, and armlets and jet necklaces were unearthed. Jet is a black substance found at Whitby in the north of England, and so the Bronze Age inhabitants of Aberdeenshire must have engaged in trade to obtain it.

Urn Burials

Gradually, instead of burying their dead in short cists, the Bronze Age people began to practise cremation. They burned the dead body and collected the ashes into a clay vase, or Urn, which was then placed in the ground and covered with earth or stones. Many of these burial urns have been uncovered in the County. At lease twelve were found at Loanhead of Daviot, while others were discovered at Broomend of Crichie, near Inverurie, and Tullynessle. Often there was nothing to indicate where the urns were, but some were found in cairns or beside circles of standing stones.

Standing Stone Circles

At one time there used to be more than two hundred circles of standing stones in Aberdeenshire. Many of these have now been broken up and others have disappeared completely. There used to be a circle at New Deer, for example, but the stones were used in building the old church manse; at Hatton of Cruden there is a farm known as Standing Stones, but the circle after which it was named has long since disappeared; and at Nether Coullie in Monymusk there is a field called Standing Stones Field although there is no longer a circle there.

At Cullerlie in Echt, there is an unusual type of circle. It consists of eight stones enclosing an area in which there are eight small burial cairns, each surrounded by a ring of larger stones except the biggest one in the middle which has two surrounding rings. At Broomend of Crichie near Inverurie, there are the remains of another unusual type of circle, which is similar to the famous circle at Avebury in England. When complete, it consisted of six stones, beside each of which there were cremated burials. It is surrounded by a wide shallow ditch which was crossed by an avenue which, flanked by standing stones, stretched to a gravel bank about a quarter of a mile to the south, where four cists were discovered. To the north of this circle there was another consisting of three rings of standing stones with a small cairn in the middle. This was similar to Stonehenge but, of course, on a much smaller scale.

Most of the circles in Aberdeenshire, however, have a huge stone lying on the ground between the two biggest standing stones. This is known as a **Recumbent Stone Circle** and is found only in the North-east of Scotland. The stone lying on the ground is often called the **Altar Stone** and is usually in the south-west part of the circle. Sometimes there are little hollows, or cup marks, on the altar stone, or on the standing stones next to it. It has been said that the Bronze Age people made sacrifices on the altar stones and that the cup marks were for draining away the blood of the dead animal. Several of the altar stones, however, as in the circles at Dyce and at Sunhoney in Midmar, are not the correct shape to be of use in sacrifices. Moreover, many of the cup marks are on the sides, instead of on the flat tops, of the stones, and so they could not hold liquid. It is obvious therefore, that all the recumbent stone circles could not have been used for sacrifices.

Nevertheless, there are several places in the County where stone circles were at one time believed to have been heathen temples. In the Temple Field at Potterton near Belhelvie, there used to be a circle known as the Temple Stones, while at South Ythsie, Tarves, there is a circle in the Temple Park, and the circle which once stood at Hatton of Cruden was known as the Temple of Cruden. In other places, the circles were called "Kirks". For example, one was known as the Auld Kirk o' Alford, while, another, on the south side of the Hill of Corrennie, was called the Auld Kirk o' Tough. Another, which stood at the farm of Tofthills in Clatt, was known as the Sunken Kirk. Yet another circle, at Fetternear about six miles from Inverurie, was given the name of the Chapel o' Sink.

As we can see, there are plenty of examples in Aberdeenshire of standing stone circles which are thought to have been connected with worship. In fact, one circle, which used to stand about a mile from Potarch, was called the Worship Stone. Nobody knows, however, why the circles were erected. All that is certain is that they were in use during the Bronze Age and that they were connected with burials since short cists or urns have been discovered beside most of the stone circles in the County.

Round Cairns

During the Bronze Age, cairns were sometimes built over the short cist and urn burials. The cairns were round, not long-shaped as in the Stone Age, and are known as Round Cairns. Many of them have now disappeared but there are still place-names to remind us that cairns once stood there. In the Tarves district, for example, are Coucher Cairn, Courtstone Cairn, Fedderat Cairn, Cairnhill, and Cairnbrogie. Round cairns may be seen at Bieldside near Aberdeen and on the Glaschuil Hill in Kildrummy.

Many legends have grown up about the cairns. For example, there is a cairn at Memsie which is said to have been made by a giant who, when carrying a load of stones, tripped over Mormond Hill and let them fall in a heap. Another story of the same cairn states that it was erected to mark the graves of men who were killed in a battle between the Danes and the men of Buchan. (See Chapter 4). According to another legend, Cairn Fichlie and Cairn Ley, on the Glaschuil Hill, are supposed to have been made by witches. They were flying over the Glaschuil with stones to help in the building of Kildrummy Castle when they were told that the work had been completed. Instead of taking the stones back to the quarry, they dropped them on the hillside, thus making the cairns.

Hut Circles

Towards the end of the Bronze Age, some of the inhabitants of Aberdeenshire were living in small villages of little, round huts. To build one of these huts the people first dug a shallow, circular hole, which was then surrounded by a ring of stones standing on end and fitted close together. Another ring of stones was set up outside this one, leaving a gap which was later filled with rubble and stones to form the walls. The floor was of clay, tramped until it was smooth and hard, or else it was paved with flat stones. Four posts in the centre of the hut held up the roof, which consisted of branches covered with clay, grass and turf and sloped down to the walls. When it was finished, the hut was the same shape as a big bell-tent, had no windows, no chimney, and only one low door-way.

The remains of some of these huts, Hut Circles as they are called, have been found at New Kinnord, Skene's Wood in Fintray, and West Knockenzie.

The inhabitants of the villages were farming folk, who hunted and fished to add to their supply of food. Around the huts they had small plots in which they grew corn, which was ground down in their querns. Some of them had pens in which they kept sheep, cattle, and pigs.

LEARNING ABOUT THE EARLIEST TIMES

Our story of Aberdeenshire has now reached a point between 400 B.C. and 100 B.C. In this chapter, we have covered about eight thousand years, from the end of the Ice Age to the end of the Bronze Age. You may have noticed that none of the dates has been given as exact. This is because no written accounts of any kind were kept by the primitive inhabitants of Aberdeenshire and we cannot say definitely when things happened. We can, however, learn roughly when certain changes took place and also some details of how the people lived.

The men who study these early times are known as **Archaeologists** and they find out about the past by digging or excavating. They do not dig in the same way as we would dig a garden or as men dig drains in the street. Instead of picks and shovels, they often use small trowels and brushes so that they can move the earth very slowly and carefully, thus avoiding damaging anything which they may recover. They keep exact notes of where they find things such as pieces of pottery, heaps of shells and animal bones, tools, weapons, ornaments, and human skeletons.

Once they have finished digging, archaeologists take all their finds to their workrooms where they examine the objects to try to learn about the life of the people who used them so long ago. From the shape of any pottery they may have found and from the designs on it, as well as from the kind of clay of which it is made, archaeologists can say roughly when it was used. For example, the Stone Age pottery discovered at Knapperty Hillock is very different from the Bronze Age urns found at Loanhead of Daviot. Archaeologists can also learn from the different kinds of tools, weapons, and ornaments. The flint arrow-heads which were used at the beginning of the New Stone Age are a different shape from those used in the Bronze Age, just as the axes made at the beginning of the Bronze Age are different from those made at the end of it.

Other scientists help archaeologists to find out about the past. **Anatomists,** by studying the skeletons which have been found, can describe how the New Stone Age people differed in appearance from the Beaker People. **Zoologists,** by studying the animal bones which have been dug up, can tell whether the early people had tame animals, such as sheep, or lived only on the animals which they killed while hunting. **Botanists** can help archaeologists to decide the type of wheat which the early peoples grew, as well as giving information about the natural vegetation.

Nowadays, archaeologists use photographs taken from aeroplanes to help in finding the sites of old buildings, since the underground remains of these sometimes show up on aerial photographs although no sign of them can be seen from the ground. A few years ago, the pilot of an aircraft flying above the River Ythan between Newburgh and Ellon spotted the site of a very old village which people who had often walked past the place had not seen.

In our next chapter we shall be dealing with some more discoveries made by archaeologists. We shall also read about things which are recorded in some of the earliest history books, so that we shall begin to deal with what is called **Written History.**

Appendix to Chapter I

The following lists, which are not exhaustive, give more examples of places associated with some of the topics of the preceding chapter:—

FLINT SMIDDIES—P. 2

Education Area	*Site*
Alford	Broomhill in Strathdon.
	Gallowhillock at Templeton, Kildrummy.
Ellon	Hill of Dudwick.
	Hill of Skelmuir.
Garioch	The Bass, Inverurie.
	Hill of Skares, Insch.
Peterhead	Hill of Bulwark, Old Deer.
	Hill of Culsh, New Deer.

SHORT CISTS—P. 4

Education Area	*Site*
Aberdeen	Avondow at Milltimber
	Belhelvie.
	Clinterty at Kinellar.
Alford	Ord in Auchindoir.
Deeside	Mulloch near Dinnet.
Ellon	Ardlethen.
	Craigies in Tarves.
	Hillhead.
	Mains of Tolquhoun.
	Schivas.
Fraserburgh	Auchlin, New Aberdour.
	Blackhills, Tyrie.
	Mill Farm, Rathen.
Garioch	Johnston, Leslie.
	Newlands, Oyne.
	Pittodrie Farm.
Turriff	Auchmill, King Edward.
	Hill of Foulzie, King Edward.

BRONZE AGE FINDS—P. 4

(Axes are marked "a"; swords are marked "sw"; and spear-heads are marked "sp".)

Education Area	*Site*
Alford	Alford (a. and sw.).
	Auchindoir (sw.).
	Kildrummy (a.).
Deeside	Aboyne (a.).

Bronze Age Finds—continued

(Axes are marked "a"; swords are marked "sw"; and spear-heads are marked "sp".)

Education Area	Site
Ellon	Collynie, Tarves (a.).
	Haddo House (sw.).
	Milton of Ardlethen (sp.).
	Moss of Tillydesk (sp.).
	South Ythsie, Tarves (sw.).
Garioch	Kintore (a.).
	Premnay (a.).

URNS—P. 5

Aberdeen	Leuchar Brae, Skene.
Alford	Tough.
Deeside	Tarland.
Ellon	Ardlethen.
	Auchedly.
	Cruden.
Fraserburgh	Strichen.
Garioch	Seggiecrook.
Turriff	Hill of Foulzie, King Edward.

STONE CIRCLES—P. 5

Alford	Midmar.
	Old Keig.
Fraserburgh	Strichen House.
	Logie, Lonmay.
Garioch	Balquhain.
	Bourtie.
	Daviot.
	Rayne.
Huntly	"Stannin' Stanes o' Strathbogie," Huntly.
Peterhead	Aikey Brae.
Turriff	Auchnagorth, King Edward.

CAIRNS—P. 6

Aberdeen	Skene's Wood, Fintray.
	Tyrebagger.
Alford	Carnaveron.
	Tullochvenus in Tough.
Deeside	Howe of Cromar.
Ellon	Bridge of Ardlethen.
	Pitlochie.
Garioch	Knockolochie, Chapel of Garioch.
Turriff	Law of Balgreen, King Edward.
	Mill of Fisherie, King Edward.

Chapter 2

CELTS, ROMANS, AND PICTS

Towards the end of the Bronze Age, some time between 400 B.C. and 100 B.C. a new people began to settle in Aberdeenshire. They were the **Celts,** who had crossed from France and Belgium. They had learned how to use iron and their arrival marks the beginning of the **Iron Age** in the County.

At Loanhead of Daviot, traces of a small furnace, which was used for smelting iron, have been discovered. This shows that iron was made in Aberdeenshire from local ore and did not have to be imported. As a result, the new metal was much cheaper than bronze, which had to be made from tin and copper taken from Cornwall and Ireland. Iron is much harder than bronze and so the tools and weapons made from it could be made sharper and also lasted longer. It was some time, however, before bronze implements went out of use, and bronze ornaments, such as the big armlets which were found at Castle Newe on Donside, Aboyne, Belhelvie, and Coull, continued to be valued for many years after the introduction of iron.

Earth Houses

Most of the Iron Age population, for example at Old Kinnord on Deeside and at Forvie near the mouth of the River Ythan, lived in the same kind of huts as had come into use in some places at the end of the Bronze Age. During the Iron Age, some huts were built on top of underground Earth Houses, many of which may have been used only as stores. Some, however, were inhabited. An earth house was like a long, low tunnel with the sides and floor made of stones, while the roof was built of wood, as at New Kinnord and at Milton of Whitehouse near Dinnet, or of stone, as at Castle Newe. Steps led down to the earth house, which was about 10 feet wide, 8 feet high, and anything up to 80 feet long. Some of these underground houses had little stone cupboards built into the walls. Usually the smoke from the fire went out at the door, which was the only opening in the house, but sometimes, as in the earth house at Buchaam on Donside, there was a stone chimney.

Most of the earth houses in Aberdenshire have been found in the Kildrummy district and in the Howe of Cromar. In addition to those mentioned above, earth houses may be seen at Culsh near Tarland, Tullich near Ballater, and Glenkindie House.

Crannogs

The Iron Age people had another unusual kind of dwelling known as a Crannog. Huts, made of wood and clay, were built on an island in a lake. The strange thing was that the island was often made by the people themselves. A huge wooden raft was floated into the desired position and branches and stones were piled on top of it until it sank to the bottom. Big posts were then driven in to hold the whole mass in place and, once the huts had been built, a high wooden fence was erected around the village. Crannogs were constructed because they were safer from attack than villages on land.

There were crannogs on the Loch of Leys near Banchory and on Loch Kinnord near Dinnet. Canoes, which had been made by hollowing out tree-trunks, and which were probably used by the crannog-dwellers, were discovered at both of these sites.

As you can imagine, many trees were needed in building a crannog. The result was that parts of the thick forests were cleared and the Iron Age people thus had more land for cultivation. More and more of them settled down in one place and depended on farming for their food. In addition to the old type of saddle quern, the Celts used a better kind known as a **Rotary Quern,** in which the top stone was rotated on the bottom one, thus grinding the meal. Besides being farmers, with cattle, pigs, and sheep, as well as crops of grain, the people who lived in the earth houses and the crannogs hunted deer and wild birds, and gathered shellfish, nuts, and berries, to add to their food supplies.

The Romans

While the Celts were settling in Aberdeenshire and passing on the knowledge of their latest discoveries to the descendants of the Bronze Age population, great changes were taking place in the south. Led by Julius Caesar, Roman Legions invaded England in 55 B.C. and again in 54 B.C. but on both occasions they stayed only a short time before returning to Gaul. In 43 A.D., on the orders of the Emperor Claudius, the Romans invaded again and set about conquering the whole island. Forty years later, they had succeeded in occupying most of what is now England and, led by **Julius Agricola,** were advancing northwards through the Lowlands of Scotland. They defeated the native Caledonians at a big battle at **Mons Graupius** in 84 A.D. The site of this battle is unknown but is thought to be near Stonehaven or near Keith. The Romans could not conquer the country, however, and withdrew to the defences of Agricola's line of forts, which was built from the Firth of Forth to the Firth of Clyde, and later, to the shelter of Hadrian's Wall, which had been buit from the North Sea, at Wallsend, to the Solway Firth.

Historians are still discovering new facts about the Roman Occupation. It is thought, however, that it was in the reign of the **Emperor Severus** from 208 to 211, that the Romans penetrated the North-East region of Scotland. Their route may be traced from the line of camps including Raedykes near Stonehaven, Normandykes at a ford across the River Dee to the west of Peterculter, Deer's Den at Kintore, and Glenmaillen near Ythanwells, and so on to the Moray Firth.

The Romans did not stay for long at the north of the Mounth and it is impossible to explain the presence of Roman relics in Aberdeenshire. Nobody can say when the Roman coins, which have been found at Aberdeen, Port Elphinstone, Cushnie, Castle Newe, Leslie, Clatt, and Alford, were lost but it is very probable that they came to Aberdeenshire in the course of trade after the legions had left. Nor can anyone explain the presence of a Roman silver brooch in a grave near Tarland, or how a Roman glass jug came to be at Brackenbraes in the parish of Turriff. On the whole, the influence of the Roman Occupation on Aberdeenshire was very small but it is probable that it did compel the inhabitants to join together to fight the invaders.

Hill Forts

Some, if not all, of the forts which once stood on several Aberdeenshire hill-tops may have been used at this time. Indeed, it is probable that some of them may have been specially built to oppose the invasion.

The remains of the fifteen feet thick stone wall of one of these hill-forts may still be seen on the Mither Tap of Bennachie. There used to be at least ten hut circles and an underground well inside the wall, which was built lower on the inside than on the outside, so that the defenders could stand on it and throw stones and other missiles over the top on the enemy and still be shielded themselves. There were six hill forts placed in a circle around the one on Bennachie and it is possible that their occupants kept in touch by means of signal fires. Two of the six, one on Barra Hill near Old Meldrum, and the other on the Hill of Tillymuick near Bennachie. are earthworks: that is, they were made by digging a deep ditch and throwing the earth up into a mound or dyke. The others, the Barmekin of Echt, the Barmekin of Keig, the fort on Dunnideer, and the fort on Tap o' Noth, were stone-built. The last two are known as **Vitrified Forts**. Big wooden posts had been used to strengthen the walls and, when the forts were later burned, the great heat given out by these timbers melted the stones so that they ran together and, once they cooled, formed one solid or "vitrified" mass. Some people think that the forts may have been so vitrified when they were burned during an attack by the Romans but we cannot be sure who built the forts, why they were built, and how some of them came to be vitrified. They are not mentioned in the earliest Roman history books and so we have to depend on what archaeologists can tell us about them and, as we have said, it is now thought that they were closely connected with the Roman invasion.

Devana

In an early Roman map, we find that the inhabitants of Aberdeenshire at the end of the second century were known as Taexali. Their biggest town was Devana, which, according to the map, was somewhere between Loch Davan and the Pass of Ballater. There is a legend that the Romans captured Devana after winning a big battle, but nobody can say if there is any truth in this story or not. Nor can anyone tell us exactly who the Taexali were. It is likely that they were one of the many tribes which inhabited the north of Scotland when the Romans invaded, and which were later combined to form the people known to the Romans, from the end of the third century, as the Picts.

The Picts.

The Roman writers did not explain who the Picts were but we do know that they lived in Pictland, which included all Scotland north of the Firth of Forth except for the part now called Argyll. Archaeologists tell us that the Picts were a mixture of peoples. Some were Celts, while others were descendants of the Bronze Age and Beaker peoples. They were supposed to have been called Picts — a name which comes from the Latin word for "painted" — because they pricked designs on their bodies with needles and then coloured them with dye from a plant. It is thought that the Picts spoke a kind of Celtic language, but the experts cannot agree on translations of the examples of Pictish writing which have been found in Aberdeenshire and elsewhere. The alphabet which they used is known as **Ogam** and consists of a line with a certain number of short lines cutting it or touching it at one side. The central line is usually straight, as on the Newton Stone, the Brandsbutt Stone at Inverurie, and the Formaston Stone at Aboyne. At Logie Elphinstone, however, there is a circular, or wheel, ogam, so that it is even more difficult to translate.

We shall learn more about the Picts, some of whom were expert sculptors, when, in the next chapter, we discover how they became Christians.

Chapter 3

THE COMING OF CHRISTIANITY

It was not until many years after the birth of Jesus that the first attempt was made to convert the heathen Picts of Aberdeenshire to Christianity. Missionaries came from **Whithorn** in the south of Scotland, **Bangor** in Northern Ireland, and **Glasgow**. They worked hard, but it was about five hundred years after the first missionary came to the County before all the people were converted to Christianity.

The missionaries usually travelled in pairs, walking many miles and preaching as they went. Sometimes they would stay in one place for a while and build a mud-and-wattle church, which had no fixed seats or pews and no glass windows. The building had no spire or steeple and, to show that it was a church, the missionaries often set up a stone with the sign of the cross carved on it. As they went from place to place, the missionaries taught the Picts how to be better farmers. Sometimes they gave them seeds with which they could grow crops. When they were not out in the countryside working on the land or preaching, the missionaries would be in their monasteries praying, or studying manuscripts, which were written by hand by some of the monks who often decorated them with coloured pictures and designs.

Missionaries from Whithorn

The first man to preach Christianity in Aberdeenshire is thought to have been **St. Ninian.** He landed at Whithorn in 396 or 397 and founded a monastery from which he and his followers made many journeys to the east and north of Scotland to tell the people about Jesus. St. Ninian established a church at Andet in Methlick, where there is still St. Ninian's Well. St. Ninian had been a follower of a French saint called Martin. One of the old divisions of Aberdeenshire was Formartine which means "Martin's land", and it may have been so called by St. Ninian and his followers.

Another well-known missionary was **St. Ternan,** a disciple of St. Ninian. St. Ternan set up a monastery at Banchory-Ternan, which is usually known to-day simply as Banchory, a name which comes from the word "bangor", meaning a "monastery". Banchory-Ternan thus means "the monastery of Ternan". St. Ternan had a very special bell known as the Ronecht or Songster, which was said to have followed him all the way from Rome, and whenever it was lost it always found its way back to its owner. When the railway line was being laid near the station at Banchory, a small, square hand-bell was dug up. This may have been the Songster but it has long since disappeared. From his monastery at Banchory, St. Ternan went on missions to Belhelvie and Slains, where, in the manse garden, there is St. Ternan's Well.

About the middle of the fifth century, **St. Machar** was working mostly on Donside where his name is still connected with some of the places at which he preached so many years ago; at Kildrummy there is Machar's Haugh and at Corgarff there is St. Machar's Well. A cross-marked stone, known as St. Machar's Cross, may be seen in Balnagowan Wood at Aboyne. Perhaps the best-known story of St. Machar tells of how he searched for a place to build a church until he found the spot where the River Don twisted like the top of a Bishop's staff. To-day, St. Machar's Cathedral in Aberdeen stands near the site of St. Machar's old church.

In the first half of the sixth century, St. Drostan, St. Colm, St. Fergus, and St. Medan were preaching mostly in the Buchan area. **St. Drostan,** who was the leader of the group, established a monastery at Old Deer. At Fintray, a silver statue of St. Medan used to be carried in procession when the people wished for rain to make the crops grow as it was believed that St. Medan could make the rain fall. The statue was melted down about four hundred years ago — at the time of the Reformation — and made into a special cup for use in the church. Although St. Drostan and his companions were working in Aberdeenshire in the first half of the sixth century, more than fourteen hundred years ago, there are still places in the County named after them, indicating the great influence which the missionaries from Whithorn had in the north-east of Scotland.

Missionaries from Northern Ireland

Missionaries also came to Aberdeenshire from Bangor in the north of Ireland. St. Comgall, who had established a big monastery there, led a mission to the County but he did not stay long. It was his follower, **St. Moluag,** who, coming to the north-east in 562, founded a small monastery at Clova. On the south side of Tap o' Noth there is a huge stone known as "Clochmaloo", which means "the stone of Moluag". It is possible that St. Moluag went there from Clova when he wished to be alone to think and pray.

Missionaries from Glasgow

St. Mungo, along with two of his followers, St. Nidan and St. Finan visited Aberdeenshire from their monastery at Cathures, or, as it is now called, Glasgow. St. Mungo's foundation at Kinnoir near Huntly is still commemorated by St. Mungo's Hill and St. Mungo's Well. Near the present church at Midmar, there is a place known as "Corsefield", which could mean the "field of the cross" and may have been the site of St. Nidan's church there. St. Finan established a church at Lumphanan, which is some-times said to come from "Llan-finan", meaning "the house or church of Finan",

Another of St. Mungo's followers was St. Fumac, who is said to have worn clothes made of a kind of green tartan. St. Fumac had churches at Dinnet and Botriphnie, where there used to be a wooden statue of him which was washed once a year at St. Fumac's Well, on the day of St. Fumac's Fair.

In our story of the introduction of Christianity to the County, we have now reached the beginning of the seventh century, just over two hundred years after St. Ninian first came to Aberdeen-shire. Many churches had been built and many missionaries had walked hundreds of miles preaching but many of the Picts were still heathens. In fact, it was three hundred years more before Aberdeenshire was completely converted to Christianity.

Later Missionaries

The work begun by the early missionaries from Whithorn, Bangor, and Glasgow was carried on by saints from these and other monasteries. For example, at the beginning of the seventh century St. Donnan, who had built a monastery on the island of Eigg off the west coast of Scotland, founded a church at Auchterless. St. Ethernan came from a monastery on the May Island in the Firth of Forth and is still linked in name with Rathen.

Many of the stories about the missionaries tell of miracles which they performed and show how the people believed that they had special powers. We have already heard about St. Ternan and his bell and St. Medan bringing rain. Another story of this kind is about St. Marnoch, who preached at Leochel-Cushnie. One of the chieftains on Donside wished to take away a big tree, which grew outside St. Marnoch's church at Cushnie. He told some of his men to dig it up and carry it away. They did so but soon found that it became very heavy and they had to put it down. St. Marnoch, who had been watching, then picked up the tree and unaided, carried it back to his church where he re-planted it.

During the seventh century, St. Nathalan founded a church at his birthplace of Tullich and another at Bethelnie. The site of the church at Tullich may still be seen on the right-hand side of the railway as it enters Ballater. About a hundred years later St. Walloch was preaching at Wallakirk near Glass and at Logie-Coldstone, where we may see St. Walloch's Cross, and, at the entrance to the kirkyard, St. Walloch's Stone. St. Walloch was the last missionary to come from Whithorn to Aberdeenshire.

At the same time as St. Walloch was preaching at Logie-Coldstone, St. Congan established a small monastery at Turriff, to the east of where the town now stands. In later years, a small dell near the site was known as St. Congan's Howe.

Some years later, St. Manire built a church at Crathie, where there is still a part of the River Dee named "Pollmanire", which means "the pool of Manire", and it was there that the saint baptised those who became Christians. Shortly afterwards, St. Devenick was working on Lower Deeside. He gave his name to Banchory-Devenick. He also founded a church at Methlick where, in the Den of Ardo, a spring came to be known as St. Devenick's Well. When St. Devenick died in 877, the work begun almost five hundred years earlier by St. Ninian, and so ably continued by missionaries from Whithorn, Bangor, Glasgow, and elsewhere, had been completed. The Picts in Aberdeenshire had been converted to Christianity.

St. Columba and the Book of Deer

The best-known missionary in Scotland was **St. Columba,** who founded a monastery on **Iona** in 563. St. Adamnan, who preached in the Aboyne area and later became head of the monastery on Iona, wrote a book about St. Columba, but there is no mention in it that he ever visited Aberdeenshire. Yet, in a very old manuscript, the Book of Deer, there is a story that St. Columba, along with St. Drostan, established the monastery at Old Deer.

According to the Book of Deer, which was written by the monks in the monastery there and is now kept in Cambridge University, St. Drostan and St. Columba came inland through Buchan from Aberdour. They asked Bede, the chief in the area, for land on which to build a church but he refused. Soon afterwards, Bede's son became ill and appeared to be dying. The chief asked the missionaries to pray for him and, when they did so, he recovered. Bede was so grateful that he gave them the land for their church. The story goes on to relate how, after the monastery had been built, St. Columba left to return to Iona. St. Drostan was so unhappy at parting with his friend that he wept. Columba then said that they should call the place "Dear", because the old Irish word "deara" meant "tears".

Many people do not believe this account of the founding of the monastery at Old Deer but think it is only a legend. It is more probable that the monastery was founded by St. Drostan, with the help of St. Colm, with whom the monks who wrote the Book of Deer may have confused the more famous St. Columba. Both St. Drostan and St. Colm were preaching in the Buchan area thirty years before St. Columba landed in Iona. Moreover, St. Adamnan tells us that the saint from Iona could speak Latin and the old Celtic or Irish language, but not the language of the Picts of Aberdeenshire.

Pictish Symbol Stones

Some of the Picts who were expert sculptors carved geometrical designs and human and animal figures on slabs of stones. Such sculpture is not to be found outside Scotland and with a few exceptions is confined to the part commonly known as Pictland. Consequently, the stones have been called "Pictish Symbol Stones" and are usually divided into three classes. Class I stones, dating before 800 A.D., are unshaped by man and have symbols such as the crescent and V-rod, the double disc and Z-rod, the elephant, the fish, and the horse cut on them. Class II stones, dating from about 800 to about 1000, are shaped and have symbols, groups of animals and human figures, and the Christian cross carved in relief on them so that the designs stand out from the surfaces of the stones. Class III stones, dating from about 1000 to about the twelfth century, have only the cross carved in relief on them.

Pictish symbols have been found carved on walls of caves, on pieces of bone, and on ornaments, but the practice of carving them on stone is thought to have been begun in the Garioch in Aberdeenshire, where many of the symbol stones in the County may now be seen. It is not known what the symbols mean. Some have said that they were badges of rank, similar to the designs which the Picts tatooed on their bodies, and the stones on which they are carved are gravestones or monuments. Others have said that the geometrical designs had some symbolic meaning for the Picts when they worshipped the sun and the moon.

It is now commonly believed, however, that the symbol stones are connected with the introduction of Christianity. Stones of Classes I and II have been found near the sites of early churches such as Dyce, Clatt, Monymusk, and Kintore. Moreover, some of the figures on the Class II stones are associated with early Bible stories. For example, there used to be some figures, which have been erased by weathering, on the Maiden Stone at Chapel of Garioch which are said to have been connected with the story of Jonah and the whale.

The early missionaries probably built their churches at sites where the Picts were already living, for they could hardly expect people to come and hear them preaching if they built their churches miles from the nearest villages. Many of these Pictish villages would probably be on sites which had previously been occupied by the Iron and Bronze Age peoples because of the fertility of the soil, and would therefore be near standing stone circles in use during the Iron and Bronze Ages. It is possible too that the Picts looked upon these stone circles as sacred places and that they would adopt them as their own places of worship. If so, and if the Pictish symbols are connected with the introduction of Christianity, this would help to explain why some of the symbol stones, as at Nether Corskie near Dunecht and Ardlair in Kennethmont, are found in prehistoric stone circles. The symbols, of course, were carved long after the stone circles were erected. It would also help to expain why some of the early churches, for example, St. Manire's at Crathie and St. Colm's at Daviot, were built on the sites of standing stone circles.

Historians are still not sure of all the facts about the coming of Christianity to Aberdeenshire and sometimes different accounts are given of the same events, but the story told in this chapter, based on old books and the discoveries of archaeologists, is a generally accepted description of how the Picts of Aberdeenshire became Christians.

Appendix to Chapter III

Additional examples of Celtic foundations:—

Education Area	Site	Saint
Aberdeen	Belhelvie	Colm
	Dyce	Fergus
	Fintray, Dyce	Medan
	Monykebbock, Newmachar	Colm
	Newmachar	Moluag
Alford	Abersnithnack, Monymusk	Finan
	Invernochty, Strathdon	Nidan

19

Celtic foundations—continued

Education Area	Site	Saint
Deeside	Birse	Colm
	Glengairn	Mungo
	Inchmarnoch, Aboyne	Marnoch
	Tarland	Moluag
Ellon	Leask near Slains	Adamnan
	Pitmedden, Udny	Medan
Fraserburgh	Aberdour	Drostan
	Philorth	Medan
	Rathen	Ethernan
	St. Combs	Colm
Garioch	Culsalmond	Serf
	Fetternear	Ninian
	Insch	Drostan
	Keith Hall	Serf
	Oyne	Colm
	Pitmedden in Oyne	Ninian
Huntly	Clatt	Moluag
	Dunscroft, Gartly	Finan
Peterhead	Fetterangus	Fergus
	St. Fergus	Fergus
Turriff	Haughs of Laithers	Caranoc

Some examples of Pictish Symbol Stones:—

Education Area	Site	Class	Symbols
Aberdeen	Dyce	I	Elephant; double disc and Z-rod
	Dyce	II	Cross; crescent and V-rod; mirror case; triple disc; double disc and Z-rod
	Dyce	III	Slab cross
	Park House, Drumoak	I	Crescent and V-rod; mirror and comb
Alford	Monymusk	III	4 stones with crosses
	Monymusk House	II	Cross; triple disc; "step" symbol
Deeside	Aboyne Castle	II	Cross shaft; mirror; ogam inscription
	Aboyne Castle	III	Cross with Celtic knotwork
	Migvie, Logie-Coldstone	II	Cross; double disc and Z-rod; horse-shoe and V-rod; shears; horseman

Pictish Symbol Stones—continued

Education Area	Site	Class	Symbols
Deeside	Tullich	I	Double disc and Z-rod; elephant; mirror
	Tillypronie House	1	Two-legged rectangle and Z-rod; crescent and V-rod
Fraserburgh	Tyrie	I	Bird; two-legged rectangle and Z-rod
Garioch	Broomend of Crichie	I	Elephant; crescent and V-rod
	Cairnhill, Culsalmond	III	Equal-armed cross
	Drimmies	I	Horse shoe; ogee curve; mirror and comb
	The Bass, Inverurie	I	Horse
	Maiden Stone, Chapel of Garioch	II	Man between fish monsters; beasts and centaur; two-legged rectangle and Z-rod; elephant; mirror and comb; enriched cross; Celtic knotwork
Huntly	Ardlair, Kennethmont	I	Elephant; mirror; two-legged rectangle
	Leith Hall	I	Fish; horse-shoe
	Mains of Rhynie	I	Elephant; fish
	Tofthills, Clatt	III	Wheeled cross on shaft within a circle
Peterhead	Fetterangus	I	Mirror; triple disc
Turriff	Baldyquhash Stone, Fyvie	I	Elephant; mirror; crescent and V-rod
	Turriff	III	Cross

Chapter 4

CELTS, NORSEMEN AND ANGLO-NORMANS

Four Kingdoms Into One

When Agricola invaded North Britain, it was occupied by at least seventeen independent tribes, but by the beginning of the eight century, and probably earlier, they had been organised into four kingdoms. The largest was **Pictland,** which included all the land north of the Firth of Forth with the exception of the part we now call Argyll. Argyll was named **Dalriada,** a kingdom set up by the Scots, who came from Ireland and eventually gave their name to the united kingdom of Scotland. **Lothian** or **Bernicia,** lying to the south of the Firth of Forth, was the northern part of the kingdom of Northumbria, which had been established by the Angles from the Angeln district in southern Denmark and stretched to the River Tees in England. **Strathclyde,** the fourth kingdom, was inhabited by the Britons and consisted of the lands around the valley of the River Clyde.

The four kingdoms often fought amongst themselves but none could gain the upper hand long enough to unite the others under it. Eventually, in 843 or 844, Dalriada and Pictland were combined as the kingdom of **Alba or Alban** with Kenneth MacAlpin as king. He and his successors often tried to conquer Lothian, but it was not until 1018 that Malcolm II, by winning the **Battle of Carham,** became ruler of the Anglian kingdom as well as of Alba. In the same year, the king of Strathclyde died and was succeeded by Malcolm's grandson, Duncan, who became the first king of Scotland in 1034.

The Norsemen

Duncan's kingdom did not include the Orkney and Shetland Islands, the Hebrides, and part of the northern mainland. These were occupied by the Norsemen or **Vikings** from Scandinavia, who frequently raided other parts of Scotland.

A party of Vikings from Orkney, led by the sons of King Eric Blood-Axe, went on piratical cruises every summer and, as a result, were nicknamed the "Summer Wanderers". Some time between 954 and 962, they raided the Buchan coast but were defeated by the natives. The exact site of the battle is unknown, but one account suggests that it was on the slopes of the Aldie Hill at Cruden.

Between forty and fifty years later, in 1004, Gamrie was attacked by Norsemen who had landed in search of provisions for their fleet, which was stormbound. The raiders were defeated and, according to one story, the skulls of three of their leaders were built into the wall of the old church at Gamrie.

A large force of Danes, led by Canute (later King Canute), landed at Cruden in 1012 and erected a fort on the links where the golf-course now is. Malcolm II gathered an army to oppose the invasion and after a battle on the Braes of Ardendraught, he succeeded in capturing the Danish camp. By the treaty which was then made, the Danes agreed to evacuate all the North-east, which was thus saved from Danish domination. The king of Denmark is supposed to have sent a blue marble slab to be placed on the grave of some of his high officers who were killed in the battle. This stone was later moved and placed against the wall beside the east gate of the Parish Church of Cruden. One account states that some of the Danes, instead of leaving Cruden by boat, went overland to join their countrymen in Moray and were involved in fighting at Memsie, where cairns were erected to mark the graves of the fallen.

According to tradition, another battle was fought against the Danes near Inverurie, where the name "Densyburn" i.e. Danesburn in Keith Hall is said to commemorate the defeat of the invaders at a ford in the River Don below Kinkell.

Aberdeen itself did not escape from the attacks of the Norsemen. As an old saga says of a raid in 1151:

> " I heard the overthrow of the people
> The clash of broken arms was loud
> The king destroyed the peace
> Of the dwellers in Apardion."

In spite of all the raids, however, there does not seem to have been any permanent Norse settlement in Aberdeenshire. The area we now know as Sutherland (the south land) was the southern limit of Viking occupation. Between it and Aberdeenshire, was the semi-independent province of Moravia, which grew increasingly powerful and refused to obey the kings of Scotland. As a result, Aberdeenshire became important as a base from which to subdue Moray and then re-conquer the lands further north.

Macbeth

Duncan's succession to the Scottish Throne in 1034 was disputed by Thorfinn, the Norwegian Earl of Orkney who ruled Caithness and Sutherland, and by Macbeth, the chieftain of Moray. They joined forces against Duncan who was defeated by Thorfinn at Burghead and eventually slain by Macbeth at Bothgowan near Egin, in 1040.

Macbeth and Thorfinn then divided Scotland between them, with the former taking the title of King. He was a strong ruler and remained on the throne for seventeen years in spite of several attempts to displace him. In 1057, Malcolm Canmore or Bighead, who was Duncan's son and had taken refuge in England, made a surprise attack on Macbeth, who fled north towards Aboyne. Malcolm's forces overtook him at the Water of Tarland not far from Queen's Hill and a running fight took place towards Lumphanan. Macbeth is supposed to have refreshed himself during the battle at what is now known as **Macbeth's Well**, and

Macbeth's Cairn, which is on the slope of Perkhill, less than a mile north-west of Lumphanan station, is said to mark the spot where he was killed.

In the following year, Macbeth's son Lulach, who had succeeded his father, was killed at Essie near Rhynie. Malcolm Canmore was still not in control of all Scotland, however, for Thorfinn continued to rule the Buchan district and all the land to the north until his death in 1064, when most of the area fell into the hands of native chiefs.

Malcolm Canmore and Queen Margaret

Malcolm attemped to gain the support of the north by marrying Thorfinn's widow, but she died soon afterwards and, in 1067, he married Margaret Atheling, the sister of Edgar, one of the claimants to the English throne. The queen set about reforming the Celtic Church to bring it into line with the Roman Catholic Church in England. She believed that the backwardness of the Scottish Church was due to the use of the Gaelic language and so she attempted to enforce the adoption of English. Margaret also invited many foreigners to her Court and they, along with the Saxons who had fled from William the Conqueror after his invasion of England in 1066, helped the queen in her efforts to make Scotland more like England. During the reigns of her descendants, English influence was extended even further and Scotland became a feudal monarchy on the Anglo-Norman pattern.

Feudalism

Most of the work of introducing feudalism to Scotland was carried out by David I, the youngest son of Queen Margaret. He and his successors continued the policy of inviting Saxons and Normans to settle in Scotland. Many such incomers were established in Aberdeenshire during the twelfth and thirteenth centuries. For example, there were de Lesselyns at Leslie, de Balliols at Dunnideer, Bissets at Aboyne, Le Neyms at Peterhead, Comyns at King Edward, Slains, and elsewhere in Buchan, Lambertons at Bourtie, and Durwards at Lumphanan. In addition, there were descendants of old Celtic landowners who had adopted Anglo-Norman ways, the most important being the Earl of Mar with lands at Kildrummy, Migvie, and Kindrochit, and the Earl of Fife at Huntly.

In return for the large grants of land which the king gave them, the **Barons** did not pay a money rent but took an oath that they would be faithful to him and would serve him when necessary. The king thus made sure of having an army, for the greatest service which his **vassals** had to render was to assist him in time of war. The barons in turn gave land to sub-tenants, who had to swear to be loyal to their overlords and to undertake to do military service if called upon. The sub-tenants also loaned out land to others, **freemen** and **villeins,** who paid their rent by giving some of their farm produce, such as grain, poultry, and sheep, to their lord and by working unpaid for him. The lowest class in the feudal system consisted of **serfs** who, owning no land, could be bought and sold in the same way as cattle and were not allowed to leave the place in which they had been born, nor to marry, without their lord's permission. Serfs are mentioned in several old Aberdeenshire charters. In 1200, for example, the king's brother gave five serfs to the Earl of Mar, and six years later, when landowners at Fedderate and Cruden exchanged estates, the serfs were given over along with the other property. Serfdom, apart from that in coal mines, died out in Scotland earlier than anywhere else in Europe and it is thought to have been abolished in Aberdeenshire soon after 1388, when serfs were sold along with land at Murtle on Lower Deeside.

The feudal barons built castles on their lands, usually at the top of a hill or mound, surrounded by a deep ditch or moat. Early castles consisted of wooden towers within high wooden stockades and it was not until the latter half of the thirteenth century that stone castles, such as Kildrummy, Coull, and Migvie were built and earthworks, such as the Doune of Invernochty, the Peel of Lumphanan, and the Bass of Inverurie gradually went out of use. (See Chapter 10.)

Castles, as the headquarters of the barons and their retainers, or armed followers, became the centres from which opposition to the introduction to the Norman way of life was crushed. Since this opposition came mostly from Moray, and since the castles at Huntly and Kildrummy and on Deeside guarded the route from the south into Moray, they were especially important and the king had to make sure that they were always in the hands of very trustworthy supporters.

The Church

Queen Margaret's policy of reforming the Celtic Church was continued by her descendants. As a result, many abbeys and monasteries were built and occupied by monks belonging to one or other of the European Orders. Scotland was divided into dioceses under Bishops, each in charge of a number of parishes. Many of the parish churches replaced churches which had been established by the missionaries of whom we read in the previous chapter. Others developed out of the chapels attached to the castles of the barons, for once again the Canmore dynasty received valuable help from the Anglo-Norman incomers in extending English influence in Scotland. This is illustrated by the fact that the castle and parish church were often close together as at Auchindoir, Inverurie, Kildrummy, Kintore, Leslie, and Midmar.

William Comyn, the first Earl of Buchan, founded the **Cistercian Abbey of Deer** in 1218 or 1219. The monks, who wore white, wide-sleeved cloaks with hoods, led very strict lives. Their time was spent in holding church services, which commenced at 2 a.m., working in the fields, teaching the inhabitants of the surrounding district, attending the sick in the infirmary which formed part of the abbey buildings, and copying manuscripts such as the famous Book of Deer.

By the middle of the thirteenth century, the last remnants of the Celtic Church had been crushed. In 1245, the **Culdees at Monymusk,** that is, the members of the early Celtic monastery, were replaced by monks of the **Order of St. Augustine,** who wore black cloaks and square black caps. Their Priory, which consisted of one dining-hall, one dormitory, and one small chapel, stood near the Parish Church of Monymusk, which dates from the twelfth century.

Royal Burghs

The third factor in the spread of Anglo-Norman influence in Scotland was the foundation of Royal Burghs, each of which had its castle, its church, and its market-place. Aberdeen's castle stood on the Castle Hill; the market was close beside it, on what is now the Castlegate; and the church, St. Nicholas, was on the outskirts of the town. At Inverurie, the castle was on top of the Bass, at the foot of which stood the church, and houses of the citizens were grouped between the meeting-point of the Rivers Don and Urie and the Bass. At Kintore, where the castle, church, and market were grouped together, the site of the castle was levelled when the railway was being built. These three Royal Burghs, which were all established before the end of the twelfth century, were founded at sites already inhabited by the native Celtic population, whose way of life was changed as a result of contact with Anglo-Norman incomers. The castle, occupied on behalf of the king by an Anglo-Norman baron, was the centre from which the town was governed and from which the Anglicising policy of the Canmore dynasty was enforced; the church was included in the parochial organisation which had been introduced by David I and conformed to the English model; and the market, which was founded and protected by royal charter, attracted Anglo-Norman settlers and encouraged trade with England.

Results of Anglo-Norman Influence

We have seen that, except in the Western Highlands, Anglo-Normans or Celts who had adopted Anglo-Norman civilisation became the landowners in Scotland; that English clergymen became Scottish bishops, parish priests, and monks; and that English traders developed Scottish commerce. As a result, English language and civilisation replaced the language and customs of the Celts. To begin with, the natives spoke their own tongue among friends and relations and used English only when engaged in trade. In time, however, the native speech died out completely along the coast and became exclusively the language of the hill-dwellers, but there are still many place-names which indicate that Gaelic was once the native language in Aberdeenshire. The clan system, which is first mentioned in the Book of Deer's reference to Clan Morgan and Clan Canan in Buchan, disappeared from all Scotland except the Highlands. The "Highland Line" was thus established not only on account of language but also as a social and political division.

The changes which were made by the Canmore dynasty took place very gradually over a period of more than two hundred years and did not cause great hardship to the native population, many of whom retained their land as sub-tenants under the new landlords. A wide gap did develop, however, between the nobles and the common people. We shall see in the next chapter how the latter, seemingly deserted by their leaders, fought under a small landowner, and then under an outlawed Anglo-Norman until they eventually won their independence from England.

Chapter 5

THE WARS OF INDEPENDENCE

Claimants to the Throne

When King Alexander III died in 1286, the heir to the Scottish throne was his young grand-daughter, Margaret, Maid of Norway. Unfortunately, she died in the Orkney Islands while on her way home to be crowned. Scotland was thus without a monarch and there was no immediate heir to the throne.

Of the thirteen men who claimed the throne, only three, **John Baliol, Robert Bruce, Lord Hastings** who were all descended from David, Earl of Huntingdon and Lord of the Garioch, had a strong claim. Baliol and Bruce soon became the leading claimants and both had supporters in most parts of Scotland. In 1290, the Earl of Mar, from his castle at Kildrummy, and the Earl of Atholl, from his castle at Strathbogie, began to collect an army to help Robert Bruce. At the same time, the Earl of Buchan, who had castles at King Edward, Slains, Rattray, Inverallochy, Cairnbulg, Dundarg, and Haddo, supported John Baliol.

The Choice of a King

The Scottish nobles could not make up their minds as to which of the two men should become king and for a time it looked as though there would be a civil war. Then it was agreed that Edward I of England should decide who was to be King of Scotland. Realising that he had a chance to gain control of Scotland, Edward forced the Scots to accept him as Overlord before making his decision. He chose John Baliol, to whom several castles, including Aberdeen and Aboyne, were to be surrendered.

The Hammer of the Scots

John Baliol was crowned at Scone on St. Andrew's Day, 1292, but soon found that, although he was King of Scotland, he could not do as he wished. He had to obey Edward I. He seemed so weak and useless as a king that he was nicknamed "Toom Tabard," which means "Empty Coat." In 1295, however, he refused to obey Edward when ordered to declare war on France. Instead, he signed the Franco-Scottish Alliance and, led by the Earl of Buchan, the Scots invaded England and attacked Carlisle Castle.

Edward was furious. In 1296, he invaded Scotland, captured Berwick, defeated the Scots at Dunbar, and forced Baliol to surrender at Stracathro. Baliol and the Earl of Buchan were sent to Engand as prisoners and Scotland was once again without a king.

Edward, who became known as The Hammer of the Scots, continued his march to the north. Aberdeen surrendered without fighting. English troops occupied the castle and several noblemen including those from Cluny, Leslie, Culter, and Keith-hall, came to submit to Edward. He then went by Deeside to Lumphanan, crossed to Kintore, and, proceeding by Fyvie, went as far as Elgin before returning by the Cabrach, Kildrummy Castle, and Kincardine o' Neil.

Scotland, however, was not subdued. **William Wallace** in Renfrewshire and **Andrew de Moray** in the north began the fight for independence. Wallace is said to have attacked Aberdeen but was unable to capture the castle. He did, however, according to one account set fire to the ships in the harbour before returning south. He defeated the English at **Stirling Bridge** in 1297 but lost the **Battle of Falkirk** in the following year. In 1305, he was betrayed to the enemy, taken to London, and executed.

King Bob

After the battle of Falkirk, several Scottish nobles continued to fight the English but they were soon forced to submit. Two of them later laid claim to the throne of Scotland. One, **Robert Bruce,** was a grandson of the man who had claimed the throne in the time of Baliol. The other, the **Red Comyn,** was a nephew of Baliol and a close relation of the Earl of Buchan. The claimants met in the Church of the Grey Friars at Dumfries and, after a quarrel about who should become King, Comyn was stabbed. As a result, Bruce had to fight the supporters of the Comyns as well as the English in his attempt to establish himself as king of an independent Scotland.

Soon after the death of the Red Comyn, Bruce went to Scone for his coronation. It had become customary for the Earl of Fife to place the crown on the king's head. In 1306, however, the Earl was a supporter of the Comyns and refused to crown Robert Bruce. His sister, who was the wife of the Earl of Buchan, decided to perform the ceremony and thus keep the honour in the Fife family, in spite of the fact that her husband was one of Bruce's greatest enemies.

Within three months of being crowned, Bruce was defeated by the English at Methven near Perth. He was forced to go into hiding and suffered great hardships. For a time, he was on Deeside and he and his followers are said to have entered Aberdeen wearing shoes made of the furs and skins of the wild animals which they had killed for food. Although he was supposed to be king, he had no control over Scotland and was even compelled to leave the country for a time to avoid being captured. The English thought that this was very amusing and, in a comic song, nicknamed him King Bob.

Nigel Bruce and Kildrummy Castle

While Bruce was in hiding, the queen, her daughter, the king's sister, and the Countess of Buchan were sent to Kildrummy Castle for safety. The castle was attacked by the English under Prince Edward and the royal ladies fled northwards to Tain where they were captured by the Earl of Ross and handed over to the enemy.

The defenders of Kildrummy, ably led by the king's young brother Nigel, bravely withstood all attacks and the English were unable to force a way in until they were helped by a traitor. The blacksmith in the castle, a man named Osbarn, heated the coulter of a plough until it glowed and then set fire to the thatch on the great hall where the food was stored. The flames soon spread and Nigel Bruce and his comrades were forced to surrender after a fierce fight at the castle entrance. Nigel Bruce was taken as a prisoner to Berwick and beheaded, at the command of Edward I.

The Battle of Barra

After winning the **Battle of Loudon Hill,** Bruce decided to try to crush the Earl of Buchan, who had helped the English against him since the death of the Red Comyn. He marched into Aberdeenshire in December, 1307. On reaching Inverurie, the king became seriously ill and, when his army moved to Slioch in Drumblade, he had to be carried in a litter as he was unable to go on horseback. When the Earl of Buchan heard that Bruce could not lead his men, he collected his followers from the Buchan district and attacked the royal camp at Drumblade. The king's brother, Edward, successfully led the defence of the camp and the royalist army then moved to Strathbogie, with Bruce once more being carried in a litter. They then returned to Inverurie, where Bruce's camp was set up on the hill at **Crichie** while his men stayed in the hollow at Ardtannies.

Meanwhile, the Earl of Buchan had taken up position near **Oldmeldrum.** Sir David Brechin, the king's nephew, was with the Comyn army and he led some of them into Inverurie to see if he could do any damage to Bruce's followers. Taking them by surprise, he managed to kill a few and the rest fled to tell the king what had happened.

As soon as he heard of the attack, Bruce ordered his horse to be made ready so that he could lead his men against the Earl of Buchan. Some of his nobles pointed out that he was still sick and in no condition to fight. He replied that no medicine could have cured him so quickly as the news of his nephew's attack. "Either I shall have them, or they shall have me," he said, and gathering his men, he led them off to battle.

Bruce took his enemies by surprise. They had thought he was still ill in bed and, when they saw him at the head of his troops, some of them fled without fighting. The king led the attack against the others and, at the **Battle of Barra** near Oldmeldrum, completely defeated them, chasing some as far as Fyvie.

The Harrying of Buchan

As the Earl of Buchan's men fled northward from Barra, part of the king's army, led by Edward Bruce, followed them into Buchan. The royal army camped on the slopes of what is now called **Bruce Hill,** about two miles outside New Deer. They defeated the Buchan men on **Aikey Brae,** outside Old Deer and the Earl of Buchan fled to England, where he died five years later.

Edward Bruce followed up his victory at Aikey by plundering the whole district. In the words of the old poem, he

" gert his men burn all Bouchane
Fra end to end and sparit nane."

They did so much damage that people still spoke about it fifty years later. Even to-day, when peats are being dug from the mosses, men often find burned roots of oak trees, which may have been set on fire during this harrying of Buchan.

Bon Accord

Several Aberdeen citizens had been fighting for Bruce at Barra. After the battle they decided to return to the town and attempt to capture the castle, which was still held by the English. The attack took place at night and the Aberdonians used the words "Bon Accord" as a password so that they could distinguish friend from foe. The castle was burned and the English garrison killed. Aberdeen was held for Bruce from then on and he later rewarded the citizens for being so faithful. When the town was given a coat-of-arms and a motto, the words "Bon Accord" were chosen in memory of the night when Aberdeen Castle was won back from the English.

Robert Bruce Victorious

The Battle of Barra and the complete defeat of the Buchan men at Aikey Brae mark the turning point of the war. Instead of always losing battles, as he had done when he first became king, Bruce was now more successful and by the end of 1308, the English had been driven from all the castles in the north of Scotland. The king then turned his attention to the south and by 1314 very few castles were still in enemy hands. One of these was Stirling and it was to be handed over to the Scots if it was not relieved by an English army by Midsummer Day. On that day, Bruce defeated a large English army, led by Edward II, at the **Battle of Bannockburn,** where **Robert Keith,** who had lands at Kintore, played an important part in the victory by leading the Scottish cavalry.

In spite of their defeat at Bannockburn, the English would not recognise Scotland as an independent country. The Scottish barons, in 1320, sent a letter to the Pope asking him to declare Scotland independent. This letter is known as the **Declaration of Arbroath** and in it the nobles declared that they would fight to the death for liberty. It was not until 1328, however, that Scottish independence was recognised by the English, under the **Treaty of Northampton.** Robert Bruce had at last finished the task which he had begun more than twenty years earlier, namely the freeing of Scotland from the domination of England.

31

The King Rewards His Followers

As soon as he began to win, Bruce set about rewarding his supporters by giving them huge grants of land. In 1309, Robert Keith, who later fought so well at Bannockburn, was given land at Kintore. Hallforest Castle, the ruins of which may still be seen, was built there soon afterwards and was often visited by the king when he was hunting in the forests of Aberdeenshire.

Bruce rewarded the citizens of Aberdeen for all the help they had given him, especially at the time of the Battle of Barra, by granting them the great forest of Stocket and, among other things, allowing them to fish in the River Don free of charge. The estates of Cruden, Slains, and Rattray, which had belonged to the Earl of Buchan, were given to Sir Gilbert Hay, Lord of Erroll, who also received the Earl's old title of Lord High Constable of Scotland. In 1319, Sir Adam Gordon of Huntly in Berwickshire was rewarded for his services to Bruce with the grant of Strathbogie, which was later named Huntly. Although the Gordons did not take possession of Strathbogie until 1376, they soon became the most powerful family in Aberdeenshire and played a leading part in its history.

A story is told that Robert Bruce, while hunting in the Forest of Stocket, was attacked by a wolf. One of his attendants, a man called Robert, killed it with a dagger and afterwards was known as Robert Skene, the second part of his name coming from the Gaelic word for a dagger. As a reward for saving the king's life, Robert Skene was given land at the place we now know as Skene, which, according to the story, was named after him, and, in memory of the killing of the wolf, three daggers and three wolves' heads were put on the Skene coat-of-arms.

In 1323, two of Bruce's most faithful supporters were given land on Deeside, and their decendants still own the estates to-day. The eastern part of the royal Forest of Drum was given to William Irvine, who had been the king's armour-bearer. It is very probable that the Square tower of Drum Castle was standing then and was given to the Irvines along with the estate. The western part of the forest was granted to Alexander Burnett, and the famous Horn of Leys, which is now kept in Crathes Castle, is said to have been given at the same time as a sign that the Burnett family were the guardians of the forest.

The Start of the Second Civil War

Robert Bruce died in 1329 and there was again trouble about who was to be king of Scotland. Bruce's son, **David,** was only eight years old and so was unable to rule. In 1331, however, he was crowned king and a Regent was appointed. By this time, **Edward Baliol,** the son of John Baliol had claimed the throne and Edward III of England promised to help him to become king, as did some members of the Comyn family who were exiled in England. Edward Baliol invaded Scotland in 1332, defeated the supporters of David Bruce at **Dupplin Moor,** and was crowned king. He was soon chased back to England by David's supporters but returned with an English army and again defeated the Scots at **Halidon Hill** in 1333. David Bruce was sent to France for safety and Edward Baliol became king of Scotland. He accepted Edward III as his Overlord and so Scotland was once again under the control of the English king.

The Battle of Culblean

David Bruce's followers continued to oppose Edward Baliol and his English allies. Their leader was **Sir Andrew Moray,** the husband of Dame Christian Bruce, who was the sister of King Robert Bruce. By 1335, however, only five Scottish castles were still in the hands of David's supporters. One of these was Kildrummy, which was being besieged by an army led by the **Earl of Atholl,** who, being a grandson of the Red Comyn, was eager to take revenge on the Bruce family for the murder of his grandfather.

Dame Christian Bruce was in Kildrummy Castle but the Regent Moray was in the south of Scotland at the time and the defence was led by **John of the Craig,** who owned the lands of Auchindoir. Earlier in the war, John had been captured by the Earl of Atholl but had been released when he promised to pay a ransom before St Andrew's Day, 1335. This date was not far off and so John of the Craig was specially anxious to prevent the capture of the castle. He defended it very skilfully and the Earl of Atholl's men could not force a way inside.

As soon as the Regent heard that Kildrummy was under siege, he marched north to relieve it, collecting an army as he went. The Earl of Atholl learned that he was coming and decided to withdraw southwards. He reached **Loch Davan** on Deeside, on the evening of the 29th November. On the same evening, Moray's army, coming from the south, camped on the opposite side of the Loch.

During the night, John of the Craig and three hundred men from Kildrummy arrived to join the Regent's army. John told Sir Andrew that he knew of a path by which they could march round the flank of Atholl's army and be in a position to make a surprise attack on it in the morning. Moray therefore divided his army into two sections. One, under **Earl Douglas,** was to remain in camp until dawn and then advance openly to attack the enemy. The other, commanded by the Regent and guided by John of the Craig, was to make a night march and take up position on Atholl's flank and so be ready to attack once the enemy had been engaged by Earl Douglas. On the following day, St. Andrew's Day, 1335, a bitter struggle took place on the slopes of **Culblean,** during which the Earl of Atholl was killed and the Regent's forces were victorious.

The Return of David Bruce

After the battle of Culblean, Sir Andrew Moray was more successful in his fight against Edward Baliol's supporters and in the next five years he gradually won back Scotland for David Bruce. Edward III invaded Scotland in 1336 and marched north by way of Potarch and Lumphanan, where his army camped one night. On his return journey, he passed close to Kildrummy Castle but did not attack it. He defeated the citizens of Aberdeen after a short fight at the Green and set fire to the town, which burned for six days. In spite of this English success, however, Edward Baliol was finally forced to flee and David Bruce returned to Scotland in 1341.

Among those whom the young king rewarded for carrying on the fight for independence was the Leslie family, to whom he granted the lands of Balquhain. He also gave money and timber to help in the rebuilding of Aberdeen, which was afterwards known as New Aberdeen.

With the return of David II, the Wars of Independence came to an end. During the fighting, which had lasted almost fifty years, much damage had been done and the land was very poor as a result. Moreover, many of the nobles who had been given big estates by the Bruce family became almost as powerful as the king. Their descendants often fought amongst themselves and some even rebelled against the king. The next three hundred years were troubled times indeed for Scotland.

Chapter 6

THE RED HARLAW

Troublesome Nobles

We have seen how Robert Bruce and his son, David, rewarded their supporters by giving them big grants of land. Some of these noble families became almost as powerful as the king and caused much trouble in Scotland. Instead of trying to control them, Robert II attempted to keep them quiet by giving them even more land. His successor, Robert III, was so weak that his brothers, the Earl of Buchan and the Duke of Albany, did more or less as they pleased. The former caused so much trouble that he was nick-named the Wolf of Badenoch, while the latter was suspected of murdering one of the king's sons. Robert III decided to send his other son, James, to France for safety, but the ship in which he sailed was seized by the English and the prince was held captive. This was too much for the king and he died of a broken heart. The Duke of Albany became Regent, but he could not prevent the powerful nobles from fighting among themselves for more land.

Donald, Lord of the Isles

One of the most troublesome of the nobles was Donald, Lord of the Isles, who looked upon himself as an independent prince who did not have to obey the ruler of Scotland. When the **Earl of Ross** died, Donald claimed the earldom on behalf of his wife, who was a relative of the Earl. The Regent, however, refused to grant the claim and gave the lands to his own son. Donald there-fore gathered an army, crossed into Ross, and brought it under his control.

He decided to attack Aberdeen to give his followers a chance of booty. He issued orders to all the fighting men of Moray and Speyside to join him as he moved towards Aberdeenshire and, when he entered the Garioch by way of the Foudland Pass, his army numbered about 10,000. Keeping to the high ground, they marched by Culsalmond and Rayne, crossed Sillerstrind, and, finding their route blocked at Inverurie, took up position at Harlaw.

The Earl of Mar

In a ballad about the Battle of Harlaw, we read how

" To hinder this proud enterprise
The stout and michty Erle of Marr
With all his men in arms did ryse
Even frae Curgarf to Craigyvar."

The Earl of Mar summoned men from as far south as Dundee, as well as from all districts of Aberdeenshire, to meet at Inverurie and oppose the advance of the Lord of the Isles. Among those who answered the summons were Sir Henry Preston of Fyvie, who led the men from the Formartine district between Turriff and Tol-quhon; Sir Andrew Leslie from Balquhain; and the Lairds of Balhaggardy, Aquhorthies, Pitmedden, and Lethenty. Provost Robert Davidson and some of the citizens of Aberdeen also joined

Mar's army, as did men from Lower Deeside, led by Sir Alexander Irvine of Drum. While on his way to Inverurie, Irvine of Drum is said to have rested on a stone, still known as **Drum's Stone** on the hill of Auchronie at Skene.

The Earl of Mar was an expert soldier, and, according to one account which may or may not be true, he decided to attack the Highlanders from three sides. From his camp at the Stanners of Inverurie near the site of Bruce's camp before the Battle of Barra, one part of his army marched across the Corseman Hill by way of Blackhall and Tempin Walls, to Balquhain. Another section crossed the River Urie to Caskieben (now Keith Hall), and proceeded to Bourtie, from where they could see the enemy at the other side of the Lochter Burn. The third part of the army, including the armoured knights, went by the main Inverurie road and crossed the River Urie at Howford.

The Battle

Three colums of Mar's army converged on the **Braes of Balhaggardy,** on top of which the Highlanders had taken up a strongly defended position On one side there was a very steep slope down to the River Urie; on the other there was a wide marsh stretching from the Lochter Burn; and behind was the land which Donald had already swept clear of his enemies. Mar could only attack up the long slope on the top of which Balhaggardy now stands.

The Lord of the Isles had deliberately chosen his position so that the horsemen and heavily armed foot-soldiers in Mar's army would have difficulty in making an orderly advance. The Earl of Mar, however, decided to attack and not wait for the Highlanders to rush down the hill on his men. We are told in the ballad that this first onslaught was unsuccessful and his army, which was heavily outnumbered, was forced to retreat:

> " The Hielanmen wi' their lang swords
> They laid on us fu' sair
> An' they drave back our merry men
> Three acres breadth an' mair.''

The battle continued with much confused fighting, but neither side could gain the upper hand. The Highlanders did great damage with their dirks and claymores and Mar's army only managed to withstand their attacks because of the arrival of re-inforcements. It is probable that these new arrivals had been posted on Donside in case the Lord of the Isles had chosen another route into the County and advanced on Aberdeen by way of Alford and Skene. The ballad, however, tells how **Forbes of Drumminor** arrived late on the battlefield, with the men from Brux and Edinbanchory, after having had to send home for his coat of mail! Although the battle was still undecided when darkness fell, the Highlanders withdrew during the night thus leaving Mar the victor.

Sir Alexander Irvine of Drum had engaged in single combat with **Red Hector of the Battles,** the Chief of Clan Maclean, and both were killed. There is a story that the Maclean and Irvine families exchanged swords for many years on the anniversary of the battle, in memory of the great duel between the two men. Among the many others who were killed were the six sons of Sir Andrew Leslie of Balquhain and the Lairds of Skene and Rothiemay. Provost Davidson of Aberdeen was also slain and his body was carried back to the town by his fellow-citizens to be buried in St. Nicholas Kirk. (This was the last occasion on which a Provost led his fellow townsmen in defence of their town.) The slaughter was so heavy on both sides that the battle came to be known as the "Red Harlaw." In the words of the ballad:

> "And sic a weary burying,
> The like ye never saw,
> As there was the Sunday after that
> On the muirs down by Harlaw.
>
> And if Hielan' lasses speer at ye
> For them that gaed awa'
> Ye may tell them plain, and plain enough,
> They're sleeping at Harlaw."

The Greenlaw Monument

A gravestone which was erected for **Gilbert de Greenlaw,** one of the men killed at Harlaw, may still be seen inside the ruined church at Kinkell, near Inverurie. From this Greenlaw Monument, which shows the figure of a man in armour, we can learn about the equipment of the men in Mar's army. The man's head is enclosed in a pointed helmet, known as a basinet; his neck and shoulders are protected by a hood of chain armour; his legs and arms are encased in plate armour, except for small parts which are covered with chain mail; and the rest of his body is protected by chain armour. His weapons, a sword and dagger, can be seen hanging from a wide belt. Such was the equipment of the mounted men who fought with the Earl of Mar at Harlaw, but of course the foot soldiers would not be nearly so well armed.

After the Battle

As far as Aberdeenshire was concerned, the main result of the Battle of Harlaw was that Aberdeen and the surrounding country were saved from attack by Donald's Highlanders. There was, however, a much more important result. The Lord of the Isles had been so weakened that the Regent, the Duke of Albany, was able to pursue him into the western Highlands in the following year, and compel him to submit to the Scottish crown. The govenment was so grateful for the help which Mar's army had given in bringing about the surrender of Donald that, in 1413, a special law was passed by which the sons of the men who had been killed at Harlaw were excused from paying their feudal taxes.

The Battle of Harlaw, however, did not put an end to the disputes between the powerful nobles. In 1424, James I returned from his imprisonment in England determined to "make the key keep the castle and the bracken bush the cow." He was murdered in 1437, however, and Aberdeenshire, in common with the rest of Scotland, had to suffer from the quarrels of the troublesome barons for many years to come.

Chapter 7

THE REFORMATION

During the sixteenth century, a great religious change known as The Reformation, took place. The Reformers established the **Protestant Church** in opposition to the **Roman Catholic Church.** In Scotland, the main reason for this opposition was that clergymen, many of whom were not properly educated, were neglecting their duties and allowing their churches to fall into decay. Many abbeys were in charge of people, with no interest in religion, who used the Church's money for their own ends instead of providing buildings and clergymen. For example, Robert Keith, the young grandson of the Earl Marischal, was in charge of the Abbey of Deer, and the lands belonging to the Abbey fell into the hands of the Keith family. Elsewhere in Aberdeenshire, members of noble families took advantage of the bad state of the Church to gain control of her lands and wealth, so that the position was made even worse. The lands of the monastery at Monymusk were seized by the Forbeses, while the Gordons gained control of lands at Clatt, Towie, Birse, and Knockespock, and the Leslies obtained lands at Fetternear, Insch, and elsewhere in the Garioch.

Apart from the changes in ownership of the Church lands, no alteration was made in the religious position in Aberdeenshire during the first half of the sixteenth century. There was no attempt to introduce new ideas about the Bible or to change the form of Church services. Elsewhere in Scotland, however, the teachings of **Martin Luther,** who began the Reformation in Germany, and of **John Calvin,** who established the Presbyterian Church in Geneva, had been quickly introduced. The men who preached the new ideas are called Heretics because they did not accept the usual teachings of the Church. Some of them were imprisoned; some, such as **John Knox** were sent as slaves to the French galleys; and some, such as **Patrick Hamilton** in 1528, and **George Wishart** in 1546, became Martyrs, that is, they were burned to death because they refused to change their beliefs. In spite of the efforts of the heretics, and in spite of the fact that some of the nobles and smaller landowners had become Protestants, no laws were passed to change Church services until the second half of the sixteenth century.

The Lords of the Congregation and the Treaty of Leith

When James V died in 1542, he was succeeded by his infant daughter, Mary. Between 1542 and 1547, the English, under Henry VIII till his death in 1547, and afterwards under the Duke of Somerset, who became Protector of the Realm for the boy King, Edward VI, tried to compel the Scots by force to agree to the marriage of Edward to their young Queen. After the defeat of the Scots at **Pinkie** in 1547, Mary was sent to France for safety, and later, she marred the Dauphin. In 1554, the Queen Mother, **Mary of Guise,** was appointed Regent. She filled many of the important offices in the country with Frenchmen and sent French soldiers to help her to force the Scots to obey her. Scotland was thus under the control of what is sometimes called "the French party", which supported the Roman Catholic Church.

Some of the leading Protestant nobles and lairds banded together to do everything possible to set up a reformed Church in Scotland. In 1557, they drew up a covenant, or agreement, for this purpose, calling themselves the Congregation of the Lord, but they were commonly known as the Lords of the Congregation. They held private meetings at which Bible readings were given and the more difficult passages explained, and insisted that Protestant services should be held in the churches on their estates. Mary of Guise refused to agree to their request that the English Book of Common Prayer should be introduced to Scotland. The Lords of the Congregation later appealed to England for help and so are sometimes known as "the English party".

In 1559, the Lords of the Congregation met in Perth. They were joined by John Knox who had returned from Geneva where he had been greatly influenced by the teaching of Calvin. He preached a fiery sermon against the use of idols and images in churches, after which all the churches in the city were attacked by the mob and the furnishings destroyed. This "cleansing of the churches" was copied in other places in Scotland. In Aberdeenshire, the images and idols were destroyed in the churches in Aberdeen, Auchindoir, Echt, Kinnernie, Midmar, and elsewhere.

War broke out between the Protestants, led by the Lords of the Congregation, who were helped by the English, and the Roman Catholics, led by Mary of Guise, who was helped by the French. The Roman Catholic party was finally forced to surrender in Leith and, in 1560, the Treaty of Leith — sometimes called the Treaty of Edinburgh — was signed. All French troops had to leave Scotland; the Auld Alliance, dating back to the time of John Baliol, came to an end; and, since the power of the French party had been broken, the way was clear for the Reformation in Scotland.

The Reformation Parliament and The First Book of Discipline

In 1560, the Scottish Parliament met in Edinburgh and passed laws establishing Protestantism in Scotland. John Knox was asked to provide a statement of Protestant beliefs. This he did in the **Confession of Faith** which was accepted by Parliament. The Reformation Parliament, in which the **Earl Marischal** from Peterhead was one of the leading supporters of the new religion, then proceeded to abolish the service of the Mass, the authority of the Pope in Scotland, and practices not in keeping with the teaching of John Calvin, as stated in the Confession of Faith.

John Knox set forth the organisation of the new Church in the First Book of Discipline in 1561. The Church, named **Presbyterian** from the Greek word for "elder", was to be governed by the **General Assembly,** consisting of ministers and elders. (The first General Assembly met in December, 1560.) Each congregation was to choose its own minister, and the elders, elected from the congregation, were to form the **Kirk Session** and help him in his work. The Book of Discipline which was not accepted by Parliament, also provided for a national system of education with a school in each parish, grammar schools in the towns, and colleges and universities. Lack of money, however, prevented these plans for education from being carried out and several years passed before the sections of the Book of Discipline dealing with religion were put into practice in Aberdeenshire.

Queen Mary's Return to Scotland

When Mary of Guise died in 1560, the young Queen Mary was still in France. Her husband, the king of France, had died and so it was decided that she should return to Scotland. Her brother, **Lord James Stewart**, who was one of the Lords of the Congregation, went to France to invite her to land at **Leith**, and pledged the support of the Protestant Parliament. At the same time, the Roman Catholic nobles of the north, led by the **Earl of Huntly**, sent **John Leslie**, the minister of **Oyne**, to invite her to land at **Aberdeen**. They promised to supply 20,000 men to convey her in triumph to Edinburgh and restore the Roman Catholic Church to Scotland.

Queen Mary landed at Leith in August, 1561. Both Roman Catholics and Protestants expected her to support their Church. The former knew that she was still a Roman Catholic herself and they thought that she would undo the work of the Reformation Parliament. On the other hand, the latter knew that the queen was young and ignorant of Scottish affairs and they thought that she would depend on the advice of her brother, Lord James Stewart, who was a leading Protestant. Mary, besides being Queen of Scotland, was heir to the English throne but she knew that she would never be allowed to become Queen of England if she abolished the Protestant Church in Scotland. She therefore accepted the advice of Lord James Stewart, who became head of the government, and Scotland remained officially a Protestant country. Many people, however, were still Roman Catholic and the struggle between the supporters of the new and the old Churches continued for many years.

The Battle of Corrichie

The troubles due to religious differences were often made worse by the personal jealousies and family feuds of the nobles. Such was the case in the events which led to the Battle of Corrichie The Earl of Huntly continued to encourage the Queen to declare her support for the Roman Catholic Church. This she refused to do and eventually decided to take action against him and so strengthen her claim to the English throne. At the same time, Lord James Stewart, who hated the Earl of Huntly, was made Earl of Mar so that he could help in "clipping the wings" of the "Cock o' the North", as the Earl of Huntly was nicknamed. Matters were made worse when, because of a family feud, **Sir John Gordon**, the son of the Earl of Huntly, severely wounded James Ogilvie. Sir John Gordon was imprisoned, but escaped and went into hiding in the north-east.

In August, 1562, Queen Mary, accompanied by the leading Protestant nobles, started on a Royal Progress from Edinburgh to Inverness. When they reached Aberdeen, they were visited by the Countess of Huntly, who invited them to Huntly Castle and also pleaded that her son should be forgiven for his attack on James Ogilvie The queen refused the invitation and said that she could do nothing for Sir John Gordon unless he gave himself up to the Keeper of Stirling Castle. This he refused to do, and so the relations between the queen and the Gordons became worse.

From Aberdeen, Queen Mary went to Balquhain Castle and while there, in spite of the laws passed by the Reformation Parliament, she heard Mass in the church at Chapel of Garioch. Passing on by the parishes of Drumblade and Forgue, she crossed the Foreman Hill to Rothiemay House. Once again she refused an invitation to visit Huntly Castle and continued through Banffshire to Darnaway Castle in Moray. There she gave the title of Earl of Moray to Lord James Stewart, thus adding to the Earl of Huntly's jealousy of him. When she reached Inverness, she was refused entry to the castle by the Keeper, Alexander Gordon. Next day he changed his mind and allowed the royal party to enter, but he and five others of the Gordon garrison were executed. On the return journey, the queen avoided an ambush set for her by the Gordons and arrived back in Aberdeen at the end of September, 1562.

In the following month, the Earl of Huntly and his son were summoned to appear before the Privy Council in Aberdeen. When they refused, soldiers were sent to attack Huntly Castle. The Earl, taken by surprise, had no time to put on his boots and sword before escaping by a small side gate. He and his son were then declared to be outlaws.

Huntly collected his followers and marched on Aberdeen. He camped at **Cullerlie,** on the south side of the Loch of Skene, where Sir John Gordon and more men joined him, bringing the total in his army to about 1,000. Hearing of this, Lord James Stewart with about twice as many marched to meet the Gordons. Included in the royal army were the tenants of the Earl of Erroll from Slains, the Laird of Drum, Burnett of Leys, and Leslie of Balquhain, as well as the Forbeses from Donside.

The Gordons retreated to the **Hill o' Fare,** closely followed by the Royalists, and formed up in a position overlooking the **Corrichie Burn.** It looked as if the Gordons would win for the Forbeses, Leslies, and Erroll men fled, but the rout of the royal army was stopped, largely due to the bravery of William Douglas, Laird of Kemnay. The Gordons from Haddo then deserted Huntly and Lord James Stewart was completely victorious. The Earl of Huntly dropped dead on the battlefield and his two sons, Sir John and Adam, were taken prisoner to Aberdeen.

One account states that Queen Mary watched the Battle of Corrichie from **The Queen's Chair,** a big rock on the Hill o' Fare and that she afterwards drank at the nearby **Queen's Well.**

A few days after the battle, Sir John Gordon and other leaders of the rebel army were beheaded in the Castlegate at Aberdeen. According to one story, Lord James Stewart forced the queen to watch the executions from a window. **Adam Gordon** was pardoned on account of his youth. Huntly Castle was plundered and many of the furnishings taken by the queen to the house of **Kirk o' Field** in which her husband was murdered a few years later.

Mary's Tragic Reign

A poem about the Battle of Corrichie finishes as follows:

> " I wis our quine had better friends,
> I wis our countrie better peice,
> I wis our lords wid na discord,
> I wis our weirs at hame may ceise."

Mary's reign was indeed a troubled one. In 1566, **David Rizzio,** her favourite attendant, was murdered as a result of a plot in which her husband, **Lord Darnley,** was involved. In the following year, Darnley was murdered while lying ill at Edinburgh in the house of Kirk o' Field, which was blown up by some nobles led by the **Earl of Bothwell.** When Mary later married the Earl of Bothwell, some of the most prominent noblemen collected an army to force her to give up the throne to her infant son, James. They met the Queen's troops at **Carberry Hill** near Musselburgh, where most of the royal army deserted and the Earl of Bothwell fled. Mary was taken a prisoner to **Lochleven Castle** and compelled to surrender the throne to her son, who became James VI. In 1568, she escaped from Lochleven, went to Hamilton, collected an army, and marched on Glasgow, but was defeated at **Langside** by the supporters of the young king. Mary fled to England, hoping to obtain help from her cousin, Queen Elizabeth, but was put in prison.

The Gordons versus The Forbeses

For several years after the flight of the queen, there was civil war between James VI's Protestant supporters, led by the Regent, and Queen Mary's Roman Catholic supporters, led by the Earl of Huntly, who was a son of the Earl who had died at Corrichie. In 1570, Huntly occupied Aberdeen and ordered the northern lairds to meet him with their followers at Brechin, where they were defeated by the Regent's army. In the following year, Huntly was with some of the queen's supporters who went from Edinburgh to Stirling and killed the Regent Lennox.

While the Earl was fighting for the queen in the south, his brother, Sir Adam Gordon, who had been pardoned after the Battle of Corrichie, carried on the struggle in the north, where the religious troubles were made worse due to a family feud between the Gordons and the Forbeses. In 1571, Sir Adam informed the Forbeses that he would pass peaceably through their lands around Drumminor while on his way with reinforcements for his brother in Edinburgh. The Forbeses, possibly suspecting trickery, set an ambush and the **Battle of Tillyangus** was fought on the slopes of the **White Hill,** about two miles from Drumminor. The Gordons were victorious and **Black Arthur,** the leader of the Forbeses, was killed, according to one story, while bending to drink at what was later known as **Black Arthur's Well.** The Gordons then captured and plundered Drumminor Castle.

Sir Adam Gordon next attacked and burned Corgarff Castle, which belonged to the Laird of Towie, one of the Forbes family. In a famous ballad, **Edom o' Gordon,** we may read of how the laird's wife, her family, and her servants were trapped and burned to death.

The Master of Forbes was appointed to take charge of the North-east in the name of James VI. This made the feud between the Forbeses and the Gordons even worse for the latter had been appointed to govern the same district on behalf of Queen Mary. Forbes led an army north and, crossing into Aberdeenshire by the Cairnamounth Pass, marched down Deeside to the Justice Mills, on the outskirts of Aberdeen, which was occupied by Sir Adam Gordon. When the Forbeses started to circle the town on their way to Old Aberdeen, they were attacked by the Gordons at the **Crabstane.** The Master of Forbes was captured and many of his men were killed. Once again, Drumminor Castle was occupied and plundered by the Gordons.

The Gradual Introduction of Presbyterianism

The Presbyterian Church was organised without Bishops, and Christ, not the king, was regarded as its Head. The **Second Book of Discipline,** drawn up by **Andrew Melville,** laid down detailed regulations for the government of the Church. Each Parish Church was to have its **Kirk Session,** while several parishes were to be combined in **Presbyteries** and **Synods** to deal with local matters. Affairs of national importance were to be dealt with by the **General Assembly,** which was to consist of ministers and elders.

The Episcopalian Church of England, on the other hand, had the king at its head. Next to him were two archbishops and a number of bishops, who were appointed by the king and so in any dispute they always supported him.

James VI, who wished not only to make himself undisputed master of Scotland but also to become king of England, saw that the Episcopalian type of Church would be best suited to his aims and so he decided to introduce Bishops to Scotland. By a number of laws, known as the **Black Acts,** which he passed in 1584, he declared that he was head of the Church; that the General Assembly could only meet if summoned by the king; that bishops, appointed by himself, were to help him in ruling the Church; and that Presbyterian ministers were not to preach against Episcopacy. Eight years later, however, in an attempt to win the support of the leading Presbyterians, he allowed the **Golden Act** to be passed stating that bishops were not to be appointed in Scotland and that the General Assembly could meet so long as it was attended by a

High Commissioner to act in place of the king. Scotland was once again officially a Presbyterian country but in actual practice it was still far from being so.

In spite of the Books of Discipline and the various Acts of Parliament, it took many years to establish the Presbyterian Church in Aberdeenshire. For a time, one minister had to serve several Parishes. Kemnay, Echt, and Drumoak, for example, shared one minister, as did Inverurie, Daviot, Kinkell, and Kintore, while there were only six ministers in the whole of Buchan in 1574. This meant that, especially in winter, there were few church services in some places, but the local inhabitants do not seem to have protested very strongly, for many of them were not in favour of the new church.

The Spanish Blanks

The Earl of Huntly continued to champion the Roman Catholic Church. In 1589, he was imprisoned because he was supposed to have been plotting with the Spanish King to help the Roman Catholics in Scotland. The Earl claimed that the evidence against him had been forged and he was released.

Three years later, he was accused of the same offence. A certain George Kerr was about to sail for Spain from the Clyde when his baggage was searched. Several blank pieces of paper, with the signatures of the **Earls of Huntly, Erroll, and Angus** at the bottom, were discovered. Kerr was tortured and confessed that there was a plot between the Earls and the Spaniards to try to restore the Roman Catholic Church.

Although the plot of the Spanish blanks seems to have been invented by the Earl of Huntly's enemies, the three Earls whose signatures appeared on the papers were proclaimed to be rebels. James VI led an army into Aberdeenshire in February, 1593, and the Earl of Huntly fled to Caithness. Huntly Castle was garrisoned by the king's men but the Earl of Huntly was pardoned soon afterwards.

A Roman Catholic Rebellion

The uproar about the Spanish Blanks had not completely died down when in July, 1594, a Roman Catholic priest, who acted as an agent for the Earl of Huntly in Rome, arrived in Aberdeen harbour with a sum of money to help the Roman Catholics in Scotland. At the same time, a messenger arrived with a letter from the Pope asking James VI to support the Roman Catholic Church. The money and the letter were seized by the magistrates in Aberdeen and the messenger was imprisoned.

In 1593, the **Act of Abolition** had been passed stating that anyone who did not become Protestant had to leave the country. The Earls of Huntly and Erroll were among those who refused to obey the Act. The latter revived the Mass at Cruden and men were drilled at Crimond to fight for the Roman Catholic Church. When the two Earls heard of the seizure of the money and letter in

Aberdeen, they gathered their forces and threatened to burn the town. James VI marched north to stop the rebellion and also ordered the Earls of Argyll and Atholl, along with Lord Forbes, to attack the Earl of Huntly. The Protestant Earls were defeated by the Roman Catholic forces, however, at Balrinnes in **Glenlivet,** in October, 1594. In spite of this success, the rebellion collapsed and James blew up Slains and Huntly Castles, while the rebel leaders fled.

Three years later, in 1597, the Earls of Huntly, Erroll, and Angus became Protestants, accepting the new faith at a public ceremony in Aberdeen. The struggles between the Protestants and the Roman Catholics in Aberdeenshire were therefore at an end.

More Bishops and The Aberdeen Assembly

James VI decided to introduce the Episcopalian type of Church to Scotland once again and before leaving for London, in 1603, to become King of Britain, he succeeded in having thirteen bishops appointed. From 1602 to 1605, there were no meetings of the General Assembly because the king refused to summon it.   In 1605, some of the more courageous Presbyterian ministers, including those from Fraserburgh, St. Fergus, and Rathen, held an Assembly in Aberdeen. The king maintained that they had broken the law and they were declared to be rebels and were tried for treason. Some were sent into exile while others were imprisoned. During the last fifteen years of his reign, James succeeded in making the Church of Scotland more and more like the Episcopalian Church of England and the attempts of his son, Charles I, to carry on this process helped to cause a big civil war.

Chapter 8

THE CIVIL WAR AND THE COVENANTERS

Laud's Liturgy and The National Covenant

Charles I wished to make the Church in Scotland exactly like the Episcopalian Church of England. A Book of Canons, or rules for the Church, was drawn up in 1635 and all ministers were instructed to follow the same order of service, as set out in a new service book, which came to be known as Laud's Liturgy because it was composed by **William Laud,** the Archbishop of Canterbury.

Laud's Liturgy was used for the first time in Scotland in a service in St. Giles Cathedral, Edinburgh, in July, 1637. Many of the congregation did not like this attempt to enforce Episcopacy and one of them, **Jenny Geddes,** is said to have thrown her stool at the minister. (There were no pews in churches at that time and people often carried cushions or stools with them to church.)

Opposition to the Liturgy increased until, in February, 1638, the National Covenant was drawn up and signed in Greyfriars' Churchyard, Edinburgh. Those who signed the Covenant promised to do all that they could to stop bishops controlling the Scottish Church; to prevent Laud's Liturgy being used in Scotland; and to fight, if need be, in defence of their own Presbyterian Church. People who signed came to be known as **Covenanters,** while those who refused to do so and supported the king were called **Royalists.**

The National Covenant in Aberdeenshire

In March and April, 1638, copies of the Covenant were distributed to all parts of Scotland so that the people might sign them. This was done willingly everywhere except in the Highlands and the north east. In Aberdeen, most people were quite happy to belong to the Episcopalian Church. When Laud's Liturgy was introduced to St. Nicholas Church, there was no opposition to it and from then on Episcopalian services were held. Moreover, the professors in the University were Episcopalians and encouraged opposition to the Covenant. In Aberdeenshire, several signed the Covenant, but those who lived on the estates belonging to the Marquis of Huntly and the Gordon family refused to do so.

In July, 1638, another attempt was made to make all the people in the North-east sign the Covenant. Some of the Commissioners who visited Aberdeen for this purpose asked for the use of the churches in the town so that they could preach to the citizens and explain to them why they should sign the Covenant. The Episcopalian ministers refused this request and so the Covenanters preached in the back-yard of one of the houses beside the Castlegate, but they failed to make the Aberdonians change their minds. The Commissioners also visited some of the villages in the County but they were not very successful in persuading the inhabitants to sign the Covenant and so they returned to Edinburgh.

The First Raid of Turriff

Both sides now began to prepare for war. At the beginning of 1639, the **Marquis of Huntly** was gathering his followers to fight for Charles I and the Covenanters sent the **Earl of Montrose** with an army to prevent the Gordons doing anything to help the king. The Forbeses from Donside, the Frasers from Cluny, and the Keiths from Peterhead planned to meet the Earl of Montrose at Turriff and help him against the Marquis of Huntly, who decided to hold a meeting of his followers at the same place on the same day. When the Earl of Montrose heard of this, he came quickly north with a small part of his army and arrived at Turriff before the Gordons. He posted musketeers round the dykes of the church-yard and then he and the other leading Covenanters went into the church. When the Gordons reached Turriff to find the church already occupied, they turned aside without firing a shot. So ended the First Raid of Turriff.

The Capture of the Marquis of Huntly

Charles I appointed the Marquis of Huntly to be the leader of the Royalists in the North-east. The Marquis entered Aberdeen and, calling upon all the citizens to join him in fighting for the king began to fortify the town. Once again the Earl of Montrose came north with an army and the Marquis of Huntly's forces fled from Aberdeen to Strathbogie. The Episcopalian ministers and professors, the **Aberdeen Doctors** as they were called, also fled and many of the citizens threw down their arms. The town was thus left defenceless and Montrose's men had no difficulty in occupying it.

Next day, Covenanters from the County joined Montrose's army and they marched to Kintore and then to Inverurie. There the Marquis of Huntly met the Earl of Montrose to see if they could settle their dispute peaceably. The Marquis signed a copy of the Covenant, with several changes made in it. Montrose then returned to Aberdeen, where the leaders of the Covenanters invited the Marquis of Huntly to meet them, promising that he would be allowed to return home safely. Huntly, along with his son, went to the meeting, but, in spite of their promise, the Covenanters captured them and conveyed them to Edinburgh Castle, where they were held as prisoners.

The Start of the Fighting and the Trot of Turriff

Less than a month after the Earl of Montrose returned to Edinburgh, the first shots were fired in the Civil War. Some Royalists, led by the Lairds of Gight, Haddo, and Kemnay, attacked **Towie-Barclay Castle** at Auchterless. The defenders, organised by two of the leading Covenanters in Aberdeenshire, Lord Fraser and the Master of Forbes, fired several shots and the attackers fled, but not before one of the Laird of Gight's servants, David Prott, was killed.

The Royalists then decided to make a surprise attack on the Covenanters who had occupied Turriff. Led by Viscount Aboyne and the lairds of Haddo, Udny, and Gight, they marched during the night and were within firing distance of the town when the carriage for one of their cannons broke. The Covenanters' guards were very slack and did not discover the attackers, who were left in peace to repair the carriage. When the Gordons entered the town by the main street, some of the Covenanters, led by Sir William Hay of Delgaty, tried to build a barricade across the road but they were unable to hold back the Royalists. As we read in the poem:

> " Historians say when at the Trot,
> The natives then a thrashin' got,
> They threw their weapons on the spot,
> And ran awa' frae Turra.''

Having captured the town, the Gordons plundered the houses of all those whom they suspected of being Covenanters and made the citizens promise to fight for Charles I.

During this Trot of Turriff, on 14th May, 1639, three men were killed, two Covenanters and one Gordon, who is said to have been accidentally shot by one of his own side. The Royalists buried him in the church at Turriff, where the minister, Thomas Mitchell, was a keen Covenanter. He was afraid that the Royalists would capture him and so he dressed in women's clothes and climbed into the rafters of the church to hide. During the funeral, some of the Gordons fired their muskets while they were still inside the church. The bullets went through the thatched roof but none of them hit the minister. When the Royalists departed, a very scared Thomas Mitchell climbed down from his hiding-place, assembled the people of Turriff, and persuaded them to forget about their promise to fight for the king and to continue fighting for the Covenant.

Both Sides Occupy Aberdeen

After the Trot of Turriff, Viscount Aboyne went to Newcastle to meet Charles I, hoping to obtain supplies with which to continue the fight against the Covenanters. Meanwhile, the Gordons took possession of Aberdeen for five days. When they returned home, the town was occupied once again by Covenanters under the Earl of Montrose and the Earl Marischal.

Montrose led some of his army to attack Gight Castle to punish the Laird for the part he had played in the Trot of Turriff. The cannons of the Covenanters battered the castle walls for two days, but the defenders held out and Montrose withdrew to Aberdeen when he heard that Viscount Aboyne had sailed into Aberdeen Bay with re-inforcements for the Royalists. The Covenanters then retired to Stonehaven and Aberdeen was once more in Royalist hands.

Viscount Aboyne landed in Aberdeen with only a few men and two cannons but he was soon joined by about 1,000 Royalists, led by his younger brother, **Lord Lewis Gordon.** The Gordons then marched to Hallforest near Kintore, where they captured and plundered the castle, which belonged to the Earl Marischal. They also attacked Castle Fraser, the home of Lord Fraser, and laid waste the lands at Fintray, which belonged to Sir William Forbes of Craigievar.

The Battle of the Bridge of Dee

Viscount Aboyne next led his men south towards Stonehaven. The Earl of Montrose and the Earl Marischal, who were in Dunnottar Castle, quickly gathered an army to oppose the Royalists, who retreated towards Aberdeen and, joined by some of the citizens, took up position at the Bridge of Dee.

Fighting went on all day but at nightfall the Royalists still held the bridge and so the Covenanters brought more heavy cannons from Dunnottar during the night. Next day, the Earl of Montrose tricked the Royalists by ordering some of his cavalry to ride along the bank of the river towards a ford and pretend that they were going to cross. The Gordon horsemen rode to guard the ford, thus weakening the defences of the bridge. This was what Montrose had hoped for and when the defences were further weakened by fifty of the townspeople leaving to attend the funeral of one of the men who had been killed in the previous day's fighting the Covenanters managed to force a way across.

The Gordons fled from the battle-field and, left on their own, the citizens of Aberdeen were soon forced to do the same. Montrose's men rushed into the town and set about plundering it. Sir William Forbes of Craigievar, wishing to get his own back for the damage done to his property at Fintray, wanted to burn Aberdeen, but the Earl of Montrose refused to allow this.

Meanwhile, an army of Covenanters had invaded England to fight Charles I in the **First Bishops' War.** Most of the people in England refused to support the king and he was forced to sign a peace treaty, the **Pacification of Berwick,** which also put an end, for the time being, to the fighting in Aberdeenshire.

John Leith of Harthill

Aberdeen remained in the hands of the Covenanters, who soon discovered, however, that at least one Royalist in the County was far from satisfied with the way things had gone. John Leith of Harthill came into the town a few days before Christmas, 1639, and occupied the Provost's place in the church. When he refused to move he was arrested and put in the Tolbooth. He immediately made himself as much of a nuisance as possible and even tried to set fire to the chimney because, he said, it smoked! Helped by friends, he smuggled in daggers and cudgels with which he attacked the warders. He also managed to obtain a gun which he fired at passers-by in the street outside, vowing that he would kill any magistrate he saw. In the end, he broke out of the Tolbooth and set the other prisoners free. He did not take the chance to escape, however, but barricaded himself in the Town House. Having been captured once again, he was tied up in eighteen feet of rope and taken to Edinburgh, where he was imprisoned in the Tolbooth.

The Second Bishops' War

The peace made at Berwick did not last long and in 1640 the Second Bishops' War began. While the Covenanters in the south were invading England, those in the north occupied Aberdeen and attacked Royalist castles in Aberdeenshire. The Earl Marischal attacked Drum Castle. The Laird of Drum was not at home but his wife prepared to defend the castle. After a few shots had been fired and two Covenanters killed, she decided to surrender to prevent the castle from being damaged. Soon after this, the Covenanters plundered Harthill Castle, the House of Newton in the Garioch, and the house belonging to the Laird of Kemnay. For the next three months, until the king was once more forced to make peace, the inhabitants of Aberdeenshire had to give supplies to the armies of the Covenanters.

The Solemn League and Covenant

The Great Civil War, between Charles I and Parliament, began in England in 1642. Both sides wished to obtain help from Scotland. In 1643, the Covenanters made a bargain, known as the Solemn League and Covenant, with the English Parliament. It was agreed that the Covenanters should send an army to fight aainst Charles I and, in return, Parliament promised to make England a Presbyterian country.

The Covenanters tried to encourage as many as possible to join the army which was being sent to England. In Aberdeen, they offered a suit of clothes, two shirts, a musket, a sword, and wages of six shillings a day, to anyone who would enlist. Most of the citizens, however, remained loyal to the king, and only one hundred and thirty went south to join the Covenanters' army.

More Fighting

Soon after this, the Covenanters in Aberdeen decided to attack the Ellon district, where the people had refused to join the army which was invading England. Musketeers were sent to plunder the lands of Tarty, Tipperty, Rainieston, and Artrochie. William Innes of Tipperty, however, with the help of the Lairds of Haddo and Gight, collected a small force and defeated the Covenanters at Tarty.

The Marquis of Argyll led an army of Covenanters into Aberdeenshire and set about plundering the lands of the king's supporters. The house belonging to William Innes of Tipperty, as well as the meal mill, was burned. Drum Castle was captured. As in 1640, Irvine of Drum was not at home, and the ladies, having been turned out of the house, had to walk to Aberdeen to find shelter. The soldiers broke down all the woodwork in the castle, stole the meal and the malt from the kitchen, and killed the sheep and cattle in the fields. They also stole all Lady Irvine's silver, jewels, rings, and ornaments which they found hidden in a trunk buried in the yard. The soldiers then moved on, leaving a few to guard the castle in case any of Irvine's men should try to occupy it again. Haddo, the house of Sir John Gordon, was also attacked and captured. From Haddo, the Covenanters moved to Gight, where they occupied and plundered the castle. The Lairds of Haddo and Gight were taken as prisoners to Edinburgh. The former was executed but the latter managed to escape.

The Marquis of Montrose in Aberdeen

In 1644, the Marquis of Montrose changed from the side of the Covenanters to the side of the king and became one of the leaders of the Royalists in Scotland. After defeating the Covenanters at **Tippermuir** near Perth, he came to Aberdeenshire, hoping to obtain help from the Gordons. He crossed the River Dee at Mills of Drum, about ten miles from Aberdeen, and camped at Crathes. He then marched down Deeside to Aberdeen.

When he reached the outskirts of the city, Montrose sent in a drummer-boy with a letter asking the Covenanters to surrender. They refused. The drummer was shot on his way out of the town, in spite of the fact that he carried a flag of truce and should have been allowed to leave safely. Montrose was very angry and immediately ordered his troops to attack.

After about two hours fighting at the **Justice Mills,** the Royalists were completely victorious and swarmed into the town, causing a great deal of damage and killing and stealing as they went.

Next day, Montrose led his men to Kintore and then to Kildrummy. He asked the Gordons from Huntly and Gight Castles to join him but they refused to do so. They had not forgotten that he had taken the Marquis of Huntly as a prisoner to Edinburgh. The Marquis of Montrose therefore marched to Speyside and then to Badenoch, where he knew that he would be safe from surprise attacks.

The Marquis of Montrose and The Marquis of Argyll

When the Royalists left Aberdeen after the Battle of Justice Mills, the Covenanters, led by the Marquis of Argyll, once more occupied the town. Leaving a garrison in Aberdeen, Argyll set off in pursuit of Montrose and in the following few months both sides plundered and burned houses and estates as they marched and counter-marched through Aberdeenshire. The Royalists, returning from Badenoch, plundered the lands belonging to the Covenanting Lairds at Echt, Pittodrie, and Castle Fraser, while the Covenanters laid waste the Royalist lands on Deeside at Drum, Whitehouse of Cromar, Aboyne, and Abergeldie. They put strong garrisons at Ellon, Kemnay House, and Pitcaple Castle. Pitcaple was later won back from them in rather an amusing way. The Covenanters in the castle were awaiting the arrival of some friends to celebrate a wedding. When the Royalists heard of this, a party of them dressed as though they were wedding guests and, led by a piper, walked on to the lawn outside the castle and began to dance. The soldiers inside the castle thought that this was the real wedding party and came out to join in the celebrations. The Royalists danced past them into the castle and pulled up the drawbridge behind them, thus capturing it without fighting.

At the end of October, 1644, the Royalists occupied Fyvie Castle, having arrived after a swift night-march from Huntly by way of Auchterless, with the Covenanters in close pursuit. Montrose did not think he could hold the castle and so he formed up his forces on a nearby hillock and, for the next three days, there were skirmishes between the two sides. The Irishmen in Montrose's army charged the enemy and captured some gunpowder. Then their leader is supposed to have said, "We must at them again for the rogues have forgot to leave bullets with the powder." They therefore attacked again and captured some bullets. The Royalists were so short of bullets that they stripped the lead from the roof of Fyvie Castle and melted it along with all the pewter dishes that they could find to make pellets for their muskets. In spite of his lack of supplies, Montrose withstood all Argyll's attacks, although some Covenanters led by Captain Alexander Keith, brother of the Earl Marischal, almost managed to drive the Royalists from their defences. The traces of these defences could be seen many years after the battle and were known locally as Montrose's Camp, while Argyll's camp at Ardlogie was afterwards known as the Camp Fold.

Montrose next occupied Huntly Castle while Argyll's army took up position on the high ground at Tullochbeg. There was no battle for, although the Royalists plundered the village of Huntly, the Covenanters were content to keep a close watch on them until they marched off and left Aberdeenshire. Montrose had decided to attack the Marquis of Argyll's estates in the west of Scotland and while doing so he defeated the Covenanters, in January, 1645, at the **Battle of Inverlochy** near Ben Nevis.

The Irvines of Drum and Kingcausie

The young Laird of Drum and his brother Robert were very active on the Royalist side during the last few months of 1644. The Covenanters were so anxious to capture them that they offered a reward of 18,000 merks (£1,000) for the Laird, and 9,000 merks for Robert. The Irvines therefore decided to leave the County for a time, and boarded a ship at Fraserburgh, intending to escape to England, but a storm blew them north to Caithness. They landed at Wick where they were recognised and captured by the local Covenanters, who sent them as prisoners to Edinburgh. Robert Irvine died in gaol but the Laird of Drum, although sentenced to be executed, was liberated by the Royalists after the **Battle of Kilsyth.**

The Covenanters also wished to capture Alexander Irvine of Kingcausie, who had helped the Marquis of Montrose against them. One day, while on his way to Aberdeen, Irvine was met at the Crabstane, on the outskirts of the town, by William Forbes, who was an ardent Covenanter. Forbes wished to gain the reward of 5,000 merks which had been offered for the capture of the Laird of Kingcausie. He tried to arrest Irvine and when the latter refused to surrender Forbes shot him. Instead of being tried for murder, William Forbes was praised for doing a great service for the

Covenanters. Later, he blew off his hand when firing a gun in the castle of Lickleyhead in Premnay and the Royalists said that this was his punishment for murdering the Laird of Kingcausie.

More Royalist Victories

After the battle of Inverlochy, the Royalists were soon back in Aberdeenshire plundering the small towns and Covenanters' estates between Turriff and Aberdeen. They were joined by a troop of cavalry led by Patrick Leith, the son of John Leith of Harthill. Montrose had asked him to recruit this force to fight for Charles I. Patrick Leith had no difficulty in finding the men but he could not obtain horses for them. Then he heard that Sir William Forbes of Craigievar had camped at Inverurie with his mounted troops. Leith therefore made a surprise attack on the town, captured the Covenanters, and took their horses for his own men.

Montrose then attacked and captured **Dundee,** but he was soon forced to retire northwards again and entered Aberdeenshire by the ford at Glen Muick. The Royalists marched to Skene, where they were joined by the Gordons, who had at last decided to support Montrose. They were short of ammunition, however, and so they raided Aberdeen and captured twenty barrels of gunpowder from ships in the harbour. From Skene, the Royalists went to **Auldearn** near Nairn, where they again defeated the Covenanters.

The Battle of Alford

Montrose once more returned to Aberdeenshire. The High-landers in his army had gone home with their booty and, when the Gordons also left when they were recalled by the Marquis of Huntly, the Royalist army was so small that Montrose decided to stay at Corgarff Castle until he had gathered more forces. Having done so, he marched by the Lecht Road and Glenrinnes to Keith, where he met an army of Covenanters, led by **General Baillie.** There were a few skirmishes and then the Royalists returned to Donside, by way of Drumminor. The Covenanters followed them thinking that they were going to continue into Angus.

Montrose, however, formed up his army, which again included the Gordons, on the **Gallows Hill** near Alford, with the Leochel Burn to his left. The Covenanters soon appeared, driving with them cattle which they had stolen from the lands belonging to the Marquis of Huntly. This so enraged Lord Gordon, Huntly's son, that he vowed that he would kill General Baillie. Montrose had drawn up his army in such a way that only the front ranks could be seen by the advancing Covenanters, who swept across the River Don to attack. The Royalists then moved to a strong position on the summit of the hill and General Baillie, whose army was by then crossing a stretch of boggy ground, considered calling off the battle. One of his officers persuaded him to continue, however, and the Covenanters were completely defeated. Lord Gordon led a charge of the Gordon horsemen and routed the enemy. Nathaniel Gordon, the son of the Laird of Gight, played a big part in the victory by ordering his foot-soldiers to throw down their muskets and charge the enemy with their swords. Lord Gordon was killed just as he reached General Baillie and was about to seize him by the sword-belt. His death saved the Covenanters from being chased further by the Gordons, who gathered round their dead leader. The remainder of Montrose's army, however, pursued the fleeing enemy through the Howe of Alford as far as Tough, where the site of the Covenanters' last stand was afterwards known as the Bloody Faulds.

On the evening after the Battle of Alford, the Royalists marched down Donside to Cluny Castle and then crossed to Craigton near Corrichie, on the south side of the Hill of Fare. They stayed there for several days in a fenced camp, the site of which was afterwards known as **Montrose's Trench.** From Craigton, the body of Lord Gordon was taken to be buried in St. Machar Cathedral, Aberdeen.

The Defeat of The Marquis of Montrose

The Covenanters were now completely defeated in the north and so Montrose marched south towards Glasgow. He defeated a Covenanting army at **Kilsyth** then moved quickly to Edinburgh, where he set free the prisoners from the Tolbooth, among them being John Leith of Harthill and Irvine of Drum.

Montrose prepared to invade England but, before he could do so, his army was surprised and completely defeated at **Philiphaugh,** in September, 1645. Montrose escaped from the battlefield and returned to Aberdeenshire, first to Drumminor, and then to Kindrochit at Braemar, where he hoped to join forces with the Marquis of Huntly. The two men could not agree, however, and Montrose, leaving Huntly to continue the fight in Aberdenshire, went to Inverness. Soon afterwards he received a letter from Charles I telling him to disband his army. He did so and escaped from Scotland in a Norwegian ship going to Bergen.

Within a year, during which he had always been short of supplies and men, the Marquis of Montrose had defeated the Covenanters in no less than seven pitched battles and had lost only one. Yet, when he left Scotland in September, 1646, the Royalists were almost completely defeated.

The Covenanters Victorious in Aberdeenshire

Although the Royalists had suffered a heavy defeat at Philiphaugh, they continued to oppose the Covenanters in Aberdeenshire. The young Laird of Drum, having returned home after his release from the Tolbooth in Edinburgh, joined forces with Farquharson of Inverey and attacked the Covenanters' camp on Deeside about six miles from Aberdeen. The Royalists took many prisoners as well as capturing all the enemy's supplies.

The Covenanters meanwhile had put a strong garrison in Aberdeen, but this did not prevent the Marquis of Huntly from capturing the town in May, 1646, although he had been beaten in

CULLERLIE STONE CIRCLE

Cairn Ley

Entrance to Earth House at Culsh

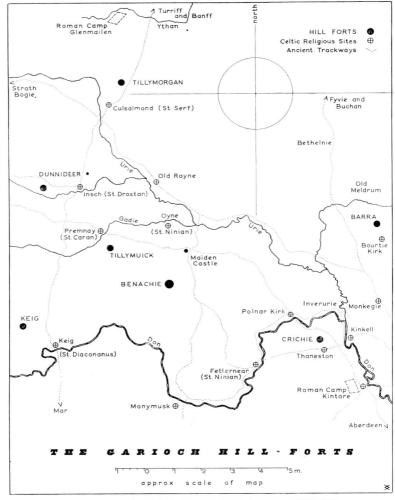

THE GARIOCH HILL-FORTS

|———|———|———|———|———|———|
  0   1   2   3   4   5 m.

approx   scale   of   map

MAP OF HILL FORTS AND CHURCH SITES AROUND BENNACHIE

Symbol Stone in Inverurie Churchyard

The Maiden Stone

The Brandsbutt Stone

HUN'

RHYNI

KILDRUMMY

TOWIE

CORGARFF

TARLAND

LOCH DAVAN
LOCH KINORD

CULBLEAN X

AB

BRAEMAR

BALLATER

MAP O

ROSEHEARTY
FRASERBURGH
NEW ABERDOUR
CAIRNBULG
ST. COMBS
STRICHEN
KING EDWARD
ST. FERGUS
TURRIFF
OLD DEER
PETERHEAD
NEW DEER
AUCHNAGATT
UCHTERLESS
FYVIE
METHLICK
HATTON
CRUDEN BAY
TARVES
ELLON
FORVIE
OLD RAYNE
TOLQUHON
OLD MELDRUM
UDNY
E
PITCAPLE
X HARLAW
INVERURIE
KEMNAY
BALMEDIE
ONYMUSK
KINTORE
DYCE
ECHT
ABERDEEN
ORPHINS
CULTS
CULTER
BANCHORY

IRE

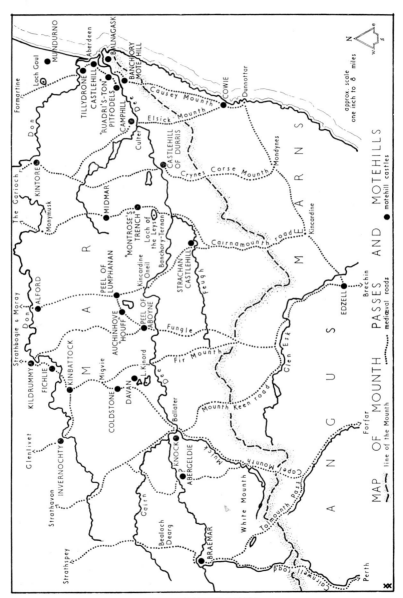

MAP OF MOUNTH PASSES

KILDRUMMY CASTLE

The Greenlaw Monument

The Corrichie Stone

THE BASS, INVERURIE

BALMORAL CASTLE

a skirmish at Kintore while he was marching down Donside. He could not hold the town for long and, when Covenanting armies under General Leslie and General Middleton marched into the County, the Royalists were forced to flee to the wilds of Speyside and Badenoch. In a short time, General Leslie had captured Huntly Castle, Lesmoir Castle at Rhynie, Wardhouse in the Garioch, and the castle on the island in Loch Kinnord, and the Covenanters were in control of Aberdeenshire.

Meanwhile, Patrick Leith of Harthill was captured and taken as a prisoner to Edinburgh, where he was beheaded. Two months later, the Marquis of Huntly was captured in Strathdon and, after being kept in prison in Edinburgh for more than a year, was eventually executed.

The Defeat of Charles I

By the middle of 1646, the Royalists in England were defeated by the Parliamentary armies. Charles I surrendered to the Scots who had been helping his opponents. In the following year, the Scots handed him over to the English Parliament in return for £200,000 and the promise that England would be made a Presbyterian country. A year later, when there was still no sign of this being done, several of the leading Covenanters, including the Earl Marischal, Sir William Hay of Delgaty, Lord Fyvie, and the Laird of Philorth near Fraserburgh, made a secret agreement — **The Engagement** — with Charles I. The Scots invaded England but were defeated by the Parliamentarians under **Oliver Cromwell** at **Preston** in 1648. In the following year, Charles I was tried by Parliament and condemned to death.

The Marquis of Montrose's Return to Scotland

After the execution of Charles I, the Scottish Parliament proclaimed his son to be their lawful king as Charles II, on condition that he made the whole country Presbyterian. The Marquis of Montrose, who was with Charles in exile, advised him to refuse the offer, saying that he would invade Scotland and compel the Scots to accept Charles as their king without his making any promises to them.

With a small force of German and Dutch soldiers, Montrose sailed to Orkney, where he made the people join him. He then crossed to Caithness, hoping to gather more support as he marched south, but he was defeated at **Carbisdale** in Ross-shire. Montrose escaped but was later betrayed to the Covenanters in Inverness. Dressed in ragged peasant clothes and a dirty old reddish plaid, and with his feet tied together with ropes of straw, he was conveyed south on a small pony, which had no saddle. He stayed for a night at Pitcaple Castle, where the Laird's wife, who was his cousin, showed him how he could escape. He refused to do so, thinking that he would have a chance to defend himself when he was tried, but he was executed in Edinburgh, in May, 1650, without even having had a trial.

The End of the Civil War

The Scots meanwhile were preparing to invade England, but before they could do so, Oliver Cromwell defeated them at **Dunbar** in September, 1650. In the following year, Charles II led the Scots into England, but they were defeated at **Worcester.** Sir Alexander Forbes of Tolquhon, near Ellon, gave his horse to the king so that he could escape after the battle, while he himself tried to hold back the pursuers. Forbes was left for dead on the battlefield, but his wounds were treated by an English lady, who nursed him until he was completely recovered.

Cromwell's army then marched quickly into Scotland and garrisons were posted in many of the towns. Some Parliamentary troops occupied Aberdeen and built fortifications on the Castle-hill, using materials from the Bishop's Palace in Old Aberdeen.

The Earl Marischal was imprisoned in the Tower of London, but his castle at Dunnottar was bravely defended against Cromwell's army in 1652, until the Crown Jewels of Scotland, which had been brought there from Edinburgh, were smuggled out and hidden in the church at Kineff by the minister's wife.

One more attempt was made to arouse support for Charles II when Kildrummy Castle was occupied in his name but, after being defeated at Tullich in 1654, the Royalists had to surrender. As far as Aberdeenshire was concerned, this was the end of the Covenanting struggles, but many people in the County remained faithful to the Stewarts and their descendants played a big part in the Jacobite Rebellions.

Chapter 9

THE JACOBITES

James VII

James II of England and VII of Scotland succeeded to the throne in 1685. Four years later, largely because of his attempts to restore Roman Catholicism, he became so unpopular that he had to flee to France, and the throne passed to his sister Mary and her husband William (crowned William III), who came over from Holland. The Scottish Parliament declared that William and Mary were the lawful king and queen, but some people still supported James VII. These were called **Jacobites,** from the Latin word **Jacobus** meaning James. The Jacobites were led by **Graham of Claverhouse,** otherwise known as Bonnie Dundee. You will have heard the song about Bonnie Dundee which begins:

" To the Lords of Convention 'twas Claverhouse spoke,
Ere the king's crown go down there are crowns to be broke."

During the spring of 1689, Bonnie Dundee was in the North-east gathering support. The Jacobites set out from Aboyne, by way of Kildrummy and Huntly, to Bog of Gight. They were closely followed by William's supporters under General Mackay, who hoped to trap them in Aberdeenshire. Mackay had ordered the Earl of Mar to garrison Braemar Castle and prevent the Jacobites from returning south by the mountain passes at the head of the River Dee. The Earl died soon after receiving the order, however, and Farquharson of Inverey, who was a Jacobite, gained control of the area and Claverhouse was able to return south after the Farquharsons had burned Braemar Castle, so that it might not be used by Mackay's forces.

Bonnie Dundee defeated the Royalists at **Killiecrankie** in Perthshire but he himself was killed in the battle and the Jacobites were defeated at **Dunkeld** soon afterwards.

General Thomas Buchan of **Auchmacoy** near Ellon then became leader of the Jacobites and after being defeated at **Cromdale** in 1690, he withdrew first to Fyvie and then to **Fedderate Castle** near New Deer. After a month's siege, the Jacobites surrendered. According to one story, there was a prophecy that Fedderate Castle would never be captured until the wood of Fyvie came to besiege it. The story goes on to show how this prophecy was fulfilled, for the Royalists cut down many of the trees in Fyvie Wood and used them in the siege of Fedderate.

Active opposition to William III was almost at an end, but many people still looked on James VII as the lawful king of Scotland. In 1692, the year of the **Massacre of Glencoe,** Lord Charles Fraser of Castle Fraser, and the Laird of Inverallochy, along with several of their tenants and friends, assembled at the Cross in Fraserburgh and proclaimed James as King. Such incidents added to the Government's fear that another revolt would occur and they increased the number of soldiers in Scotland. They decided to collect a poll tax, that is, a tax from every person in the land, and the **Poll Book,** which lists all the inhabitants of Scotland at the time was drawn up in 1696 to help the tax-collectors.

The Old Pretender

James VII died in exile in 1701 and the Jacobites looked upon his son as their lawful king. James VIII, as they styled him, came to be known as the **Old Pretender** since, according to his opponents he was not really a king, but was only claiming to be one. (The French word "pretendre" means "to claim".)

In the first few years of the eighteenth century, Nathaniel Hooke, a Jacobite agent, was at work in Aberdeenshire trying to enlist help for the Pretender, who was then living in France. Hooke received the promises of several leading County Jacobites, including the Marquis of Huntly and the Earl of Erroll, to join in a rebellion to put James on the throne. In 1707, he laid plans for a landing to be made on the Buchan coast by French soldiers, who were to assist in this rebellion. The Earl of Erroll sent a skipper from Aberdeen to act as pilot with the invasion fleet from France.

The fleet eventually sailed in 1708, without the Aberdeen pilot, and arrived in the Firth of Forth. Some British ships appeared and the French commander would not risk a landing. A storm arose and the fleet returned to France, without any effort having been made to land in Scotland. So ended the first attempt to put the Old Pretender on the throne.

The Wee Wee German Lairdie

Queen Anne died in 1714 and was succeeded by her cousin, **George,** the ruler of the small state of **Hanover** in Germany. (This Hanoverian Succession had been arranged in the **Act of Settlement,** in 1701, without the consent of the Scottish Parliament). Before the magistrates in Aberdeen could proclaim the new king, a procession of young men, led by two fiddlers playing Jacobite tunes, marched through the town to the Castlegate, where they openly announced their support for James VIII. The Jacobites elsewhere were slow to act, however, and George was crowned king of Britain.

Several leading Jacobites in England and Scotland then set about making plans for putting the Old Pretender on the throne in place of the "wee wee German lairdie", as the king was nicknamed in a Jacobite song of the time. In Aberdeenshire, the Marquis of Huntly is said to have collected about 600 horses for a troop of cavalry, as well as arms and clothing for his followers.

Bobbing John

The Earl of Mar finally decided to begin a Jacobite rebellion in 1715. He had changed sides so often that he was nicknamed "Bobbing John", and several prominent Jacobites did not trust him. Nevertheless, he returned to Aberdeenshire to gather an army to fight for James VIII.

Leaving London in a coal boat, Mar sailed in disguise to Elie in Fife and proceeded overland to Kildrummy Castle. He summoned the leading Jacobites to Aboyne for a tinchal, or great hunting party. This, of course, was to hide the fact that they were meeting to discuss the plans for the rebellion. Among those who came to Mar's hunting party were the Marquis of Huntly, the Earl Marischal, and the Earl of Erroll. The hunt went through Glen Cluny and the Glen of Quoich, where, in a big bowl-like hollow in a rock, which is still known as **Mar's Punch Bowl**, the hunters made punch and drank to the success of the rebellion which was about to begin.

On 6th September, 1715, the Jacobite standard was raised at **Braemar,** on the site now occupied by the **Invercauld Arms Hotel.** Two silk ribbons were attached to the standard, on top of which was a gilt ball, which fell off as the standard was being raised. This was taken by the onlookers to be a sign of bad luck but, nevertheless, the Fifteen Rebellion started. As the song says:

> " The standard on the Braes o' Mar,
> Is up and streaming rarely;
> The gathering pipe on Lochnagar
> Is sounding lang and sairly."

The Proclamation of James VIII.

A party of Jacobites, led by the Earl Marischal, occupied Aberdeen and the Old Pretender was proclaimed king. He was also proclaimed in Peterhead, where a mob, urged on by the minister of St. Fergus, assembled at the Market Cross to hear Bailie Thomas Arbuthnot reading the proclamation. The town was fortified in case the Royalists should attack it. Several old guns, taken from the Spanish ship, St. Michael, which was sunk at the time of the Armada, were set up on the green outside the Tolbooth. A town guard, including ten women, was organised and armed with swords and guns. At Fraserburgh, Lord Saltoun would not allow money to be collected for the Jacobite army and he also refused to turn out the ministers who continued to pray for George I, as had happened at Aberdeen and other places. In spite of Lord Saltoun's opposition, several men from Peterhead went to the Town Cross in Fraserburgh and proclaimed James VIII. They then searched the town for arms and ammunition and took all they could find for the use of the Jacobites. Later, a party of Jacobites, led by Irvine of Crimond, captured Lord Saltoun and forced him to go south to join the rebels at Perth. Fraserburgh was occupied by a Jacobite garrison, which compelled the inhabitants to contribute towards the payment of the soldiers.

Preston and Sheriffmuir

The Earl of Mar led his army from Braemar to Perth, where he was joined by re-inforcements from the Highlands and the North-east. From Aberdeenshire, John Farquharson of Invercauld arrived with a regiment recruited on Deeside, while Black Jock of Inverernan came with the tenants of the Kildrummy district. The Marquis of Huntly led his men from Strathbogie, with Gordon of Glenbuchat in command of the foot-soldiers. The Earl of Kintore, Sir Alexander Irvine of Drum, James Fraser of Lonmay, William Fraser of Inverallochy, Lord Pitsligo, George Cumine of Pitullie, the Earl of Erroll, and the Earl Marischal were all in the Jacobite camp at Perth, having taken men with them to add to the ever-growing army, which soon numbered about 12,000. Opposing the Jacobites was a much smaller Royalist army, under the **Duke of Argyll,** but Mar soon showed that he was not a good general and failed to take advantage of his superior strength.

About a month after reaching Perth, the Earl of Mar sent a part of his army, including the Deeside and Donside men, across the Firth of Forth to link up with the Jacobites in the south. After an unsuccessful attack on Edinburgh, they joined the Jacobites under **General Forster** at Kelso, and invaded England by the west coast route. When they reached Preston they were completely defeated, most of them being killed or taken prisoner.

While the Jacobites remained in Perth, the Royalists were gradually increasing their forces and so the longer Mar delayed his attack the less chance he had of winning. At last he advanced to Auchterarder, with the intention of crossing the Forth and continuing south. Argyll took up position at Sheriffmuir and the Jacobites attacked, on the same day as their comrades were defeated at Preston. After a day of confused fighting, both sides withdrew. The minister of Crathie Church later composed some comical verses about the Battle of Sheriffmuir showing just how indecisive it was:

" There's some say that we wan,
　　Some say that they wan,
　　Some say that nane wan at a' man,
　　But one thing I'm sure
　　That at Sheriffmuir
　　A battle there was, which I saw man.
　　An' we ran an' they ran, an' they ran an' we ran
　　An' we ran an' they ran awa' man! "

As a result of the battle, the Jacobite march to the south was stopped and Mar retired to Perth. The Earl of Kintore is said to have been so disappointed at the outcome of the battle that he never shaved again! The Marquis of Huntly, on the other hand, prepard to make a separate peace with the Royalists. Although an indecisive battle, Sheriffmuir marked the beginning of the end of the second attempt to put the Old Pretender on the throne.

The Old Pretender at Peterhead.

Meanwhile the Old Pretender had still not arrived to lead his supporters, but at last, disguised as a seaman, he sailed from Dunkirk in a small fishing boat and reached Peterhead on 22nd December, 1715. As it was a very dark night and the tide was out, the boat had some difficulty in making a landing, but eventually

James was safely ashore and, having been welcomed by Bailie Arbuthnot, he spent the night in a house at the Broad Street end of the Longate. Next day, still in disguise, he went by way of Buchanhaven to Inverugie Castle and spent the night at Newburgh. He passed through Aberdeen on his way to Fetteresso Castle, where he was met by the Earl of Mar, the Earl Marischal, and other Jacobite leaders. He then went south to join his army at Perth.

The End of The Fifteen Rebellion

The Pretender was too late in coming to Scotland. The Jacobites had lost their chance and at the end of January, 1716, they began to withdraw from Perth. The Duke of Argyll's army followed them north but the Old Pretender and Bobbing John managed to escape by ship from Montrose. Argyll's men entered Aberdeen on the day after the Jacobites left, but did not go any further. Led now by the Earl Marischal, the Jacobites marched by Inverurie, Huntly, and Keith to Strathspey and Badenoch, where they disbanded after the Marquis of Huntly had refused to give them any help.

Having crushed the rebellion, the Government set about punishing the Jacobites. Some of those who had been captured were imprisoned in Carlisle Castle, where several were executed. Others were sent overseas to work as slaves in the American colonies. A few, including the Marquis of Huntly, Gordon of Glenbuchat, Farquharson of Invercauld, and Irvine of Drum, were pardoned and allowed to return home. Many of the leaders, however, amongst them the Earl Marischal and Lord Pitsligo, went into hiding until they could escape overseas from Fraserburgh, Peterhead, or Banff. When about to board a boat to escape, Lord Fraser of Castle Fraser was killed by falling over a cliff at Pennan. Many Episcopalian ministers, including those at Coull, Rhynie, Slains, Cairnie, Keig, and Pitsligo were turned out of their churches because they refused to pray for George I. The people were forbidden to carry arms and government troops were quartered in several places. The Castleton of Braemar was burned and Kildrummy Castle partly destroyed. The estates belonging to the Earl of Mar and the Earl Marischal were sold. By such severe measures did the government hope to prevent another Jacobite rebellion.

Glenshiel

Many Jacobites still wished, however, to put James VIII on the throne. Some of those who had escaped in 1716, including the Earl Marischal, began to plan another rebellion with help from Spain. The invasion fleet sailed in 1719 but, due to a storm, it was scattered and only 300 Spanish soldiers reached the Isle of Lewis, from which they crossed to the mainland. Many clansmen refused to join the rebellion until more help arrived from Spain. The small force of Scots and Spaniards was attacked by the Royalists in Glenshiel and, after a day of fierce fighting, the Spaniards surrendered while the Scots escaped from the battlefield. The Earl Marischal and his brother made their way to Peterhead and escaped overseas. The fourth attempt to restore the Stewarts had thus ended in failure.

Bonnie Prince Charlie

France was at war with Britain in 1744 and it was planned to send a French army to assist in a Jacobite rebellion in Scotland. The leader of the invading force was to be **Charles Edward Stewart**, the Old Pretender's son, who is better known as **Bonnie Prince Charlie** or the **Young Chevalier**. The French fleet was scattered by a gale, however, and the invasion was cancelled.

In the following year, accompanied by a few companions, Prince Charlie sailed for Scotland with the intention of leading another Jacobite rebellion. He landed at Eriskay in the Outer Hebrides, crossed to **Moidart** on the mainland, and proceeded to **Glenfinnan,** where he raised his standard and set about collecting an army, mostly of Roman Catholic clansmen.

When news of the Young Chevalier's landing reached Aberdeen, preparations were made to defend it against the Jacobites, for Gordon of Glenbuchat was busy in Banffshire and the Strathbogie district of Aberdeenshire forcing as many as possible to join in the rising, but he made no attempt to attack the town.

Johnnie Cope

Meanwhile, Bonnie Prince Charlie marched by way of Perth to Edinburgh, gathering recruits as he went. A Royalist army under **Sir John Cope** was sent to oppose him but it missed the Jacobites and went to Inverness. The Royalists then marched by way of Fochabers, Cullen, Banff, Turriff, and Oldmeldrum to Aberdeen, where they camped on the Dove-Cot Brae, which is now Union Terrace. It is said that Cope exercised his troops at Cope's Butts, to the north of Parkhill House.

The Royalists sailed from Aberdeen to **Dunbar** and then marched to **Prestonpans,** where they were defeated by Bonnie Prince Charlie and his Highlanders. With this victory, about which the song "'Hey Johnnie Cope, Are Ye Waukin' Yet?'" was composed, the Jacobites were in control of Scotland and it looked, for a short time, as though the rebellion would succeed.

Help for the Young Chevalier

After the Battle of Prestonpans, the Jacobites in Aberdeenshire became very active. Some of them entered Aberdeen and forced the Provost to accompany them to the Market Cross, where they proclaimed James VIII as King and Prince Charlie as Regent. They searched the town for arms and, having compelled the inhabitants to give up their horses, continued south to join the Chevalier in Edinburgh.

Landowners at various places gathered support for the rebellion. While the Farquharsons raised the men of Upper Deeside, Irvine of Drum and Menzies of Pitfodels collected their followers on Lower Deeside. In Buchan, **Lord Pitsligo** was active in persuading men to join the Prince's army. Among those who went with him to Edinburgh were Charles Cumine of Kininmonth and William Cumine of Pitullie, as well as a company of foot-soldiers recruited from young apprentices in Aberdeen. George Cumine of Pitullie was prevented from accompanying them because his foot was burned when his wife, anxious to keep him at home, told a servant to pour boiling water into his boot, just as he was putting it on!

Lord Lewis Gordon, a son of the Marquis of Huntly who was in the 1715 rebellion, was appointed leader of all the Jacobites in the North-east. When several ships arrived at Aberdeen and Peterhead with men, money, and weapons from France and Spain to help the Jacobites, he made sure that they were quickly un-loaded and the men and materials sent south. He also appointed **tax-collectors for the County** to obtain as much money as possible for the Young Chevalier.

The Battle of Inverurie

The Royalists in the north — the **Grants, Macleods,** and **Munros** from Speyside and beyond — planned to assemble at Inverurie and then attack Aberdeen. While the Macleods went by way of Banff, Turriff, and Oldmeldrum, the Grants and Munros were to meet at Keith and then proceed by way of Huntly. The Grants, however, turned back at Keith and so only the Macleods and Munros, about 700 in all, reached Inverurie. Some stayed in the town, while others were billeted in surrounding farms, and were thus not in a position to meet a surprise attack.

A letter had been sent to the chief of the Macleods to inform him that the Grants had returned home. It fell into the hands of Jacobite supporters at Turriff and they sent word of the change in the Royalist position to Aberdeen.

When he heard that there were so few Royalists at Inverurie Lord Lewis Gordon planned to attack them. He led one column, including the Aboyne battalion under Farquharson of Monaltrie, by the Brig o' Balgownie and Fintray, while Gordon of Avochie led the other by the main road through Kintore. The sun had set by the time they came within sight of Inverurie, but it was decided to attempt a surprise attack. Although the Royalists controlled the fords across the Rivers Urie and Don, they failed to take advantage of this as they were unable to collect all their forces in time to prevent the Jacobites crossing. Lord Lewis Gordon led his men across the River Urie at Mill of Keith Hall, suffering a few casualties as he did so, and joined with the other column, which had successfully forded the River Don. After a short fight in moonlight, the Macleods and Munros were heavily defeated and the Jacobites thus remained in full control of Aberdeenshire.

To Derby and Back

Prince Charlie had meanwhile invaded England, but few Englishmen rose in support of the rebellion. Moreover, many Highlanders had returned home with their booty and, by the time the Jacobites reached Derby, some of their commanders thought that they were not strong enough to continue their march on London, their main objective. After a great deal of arguing and quarrelling, it was decided to return to Scotland.

The Jacobites won the **Battle of Falkirk** in January, 1746, but continued their withdrawal, followed by a Royalist army led by the **Duke of Cumberland.** The Prince went with one column of his army by the Highland road from Perth to Inverness. A second column marched to Ballater and then on by Tarland, Glenkindie, Kildrummy, Lumsden, Rhynie, and Huntly to Keith. The third column went by the coast road to Aberdeen, where it was split into two sections, one of which went by Donside to Huntly and so on to Keith, and the other by Ellon, Peterhead, Old Deer, New Pitsligo, and Banff. By the last week in February, Aberdeen was clear of Jacobites and the Royalists were in control.

Butcher Cumberland

During the month of March, in spite of heavy snow-storms, Royalist troops from Aberdeen occupied various places in the County. One force marched through Monymusk and Tarland to Corgarff Castle, where the Jacobites had a store of weapons and ammunition. The Royalists confiscated these, but the local inhabitants drove off all the horses in the district and so Cumberland's men were unable to carry their booty back to Aberdeen and had to destroy it. Other sections of the Royalist army occupied Inverurie, Oldmeldrum, and Huntly.

When the snow melted sufficiently, the Royalists continued their march to Inverness. Before they left Aberdeen, however, the newly-built **Robert Gordon's Hospital** (now Robert Gordon's College) was converted into a fort with an encircling trench and a rampart surmounted by a fence. It was re-named **Fort Cumberland** and some Aberdonians were enlisted to act as guards during the absence of the Royalists.

The Duke of Cumberland, who had been lodging in **Provost Skene's House** during his stay in Aberdeen, led his army across the River Don by the Brig o' Balgownie and went by way of Oldmeldrum to Balquhain Castle, which he ordered his men to burn. According to one story, an old servant in the castle offered the soldiers all his savings if they would spare the building. They therefore carried bundles of straw inside and set fire to them so that smoke poured from the windows as the Duke went past, but the castle was not completely destroyed. The Royalists continued by the old road past Chapel of Seggat and then through the grounds of Fyvie Castle to Auchterless, Turriff, King Edward, and Banff to meet the rest of their army and proceed to Inverness.

The Jacobites were completely defeated at **Culloden** about six miles from Inverness, on 16th April, 1746. The Duke of Cumberland ordered his men to have no mercy on the enemy and was nicknamed "Butcher Cumberland" because of his severity. Charles Fraser of Inverallochy was one of the many wounded men who were killed while lying on the battlefield. The Duke ordered one of his officers, a man named **Wolfe,** to kill Fraser, but he refused and so Cumberland then commanded a private soldier to commit the murder. (Wolfe later became a General and led the army which captured Quebec and added Canada to the British Empire.)

After Culloden

The Royalist victory at Culloden put an end to the rebellion. About a hundred of the captive Jacobite leaders were executed and in 1746 a **Disarming Act** was passed making it illegal for Scots people to carry weapons, to wear the tartan, and to play the bag-pipes. In the following year, the Highland Clan system was abolished and so the chiefs were no longer able to force their clans-men to follow them to war. The government thus lessened the possibility of another Jacobite rebellion.

Many Jacobites made their way back to Aberdeenshire after Culloden and hid, especially in Strathbogie, Deeside, Upper Don-side, and Buchan, until they could escape overseas. Although the minister in each parish was ordered to give an account of all his parishioners and to warn them against helping anyone to hide, few of those who were lurking were caught.

One unfortunate fugitive was Charles Gordon, the Laird of Terpersie in Tullynessle. While hiding in the hills he visited his home one night and was betrayed by a spy from Kintore. Govern-ment troops caught him, but they were not sure of his identity and so they led Gordon to a farm where his family were staying. As soon as the children saw him, they ran forward shouting, " Daddy! Daddy! " The soldiers thus confirmed that he was the Laird of Terpersie and he was executed.

Most of the Jacobites were more fortunate and, after many adventures and narrow escapes, were pardoned and allowed to return home to find, in many cases, that their house and lands had been burned and plundered. One of these was Patrick Duguid of Auchinhove, Lumphanan. When he was hiding on the hill of Coull, Royalist soldiers were living in his house while they searched for him. One night their captain heard a noise in a bedroom and rushed in, thinking that Duguid had returned, but he found only Duguid's five-year-old son, James. The captain offered the child his cocked hat and feathers if he would shout, "Hurrah for King George." James Duguid replied, "Na, na, I'm a Prince's man! " The Royalists later burned the house, without giving any warning, and Mrs. Duguid and the children had to escape by a window and flee to the hill-side.

James Innes of Balnacraig was more fortunate, for when the Redcoats came to search for him, with orders to burn the house if they could not find him, his wife killed all her hens and gave the Royalists such a feast that they departed without even looking for him.

On Donside, Farquharson of Allargue lurked on Craig Cluny and Forbes of Skellater in a birchwood on the hill of Delhandy. Jonathan Forbes of Brux managed to stay free in spite of many searches by troops from Alford and Corgarff. He is said to have hidden frequently in caves on Coliochvar and passed the time, well disguised, in building dry-stane dykes, some of the stones from which were later built into Brux Lodge. When soldiers once asked him if he had seen the Laird of Brux, he replied, "He wis at hame fin I wis at ma brakfast! "

The most famous lurking Jacobite in the Buchan district was Lord Pitsligo, who hid sometimes on Mormond Hill, sometimes under the old bridge at Craigmaud, New Pitsligo, and sometimes in a cave at Cowshaven (afterwards known as Lord Pitsligo's Cave) about two miles from Rosehearty. Dressed as a beggar, he once received money from Redcoats and then led them to search his cave. At another time, he held a lantern so that Royalists could search a house in which he was supposed to be hiding. On another occasion, while he was staying at Auchiries, troops arrived during the night to look for him. Lord Pitsligo hid behind the wooden panelling in a bedroom occupied by a young girl. He had a fit of asthma while the soldiers were in the room and, to cover the noise of his breathing, the girl pretended to have a bad cough and he was not discovered.

Other well-known Jacobites who eventually escaped to Norway from Buchan were Gordon of Glenbuchat and Moir of Stoneywood. The former owned the house known as "The Warld's End", which is still standing near the railway station in Fraserburgh.

Although all the Jacobite rebellions had ended in failure, many people still regarded the Stewarts as the Royal Family. Songs were composed expressing their loyalty, typical of them being the following verse from a song in which the ferryman at Waterside of Birse near Aboyne is mentioned:

" Come boat me o'er, come row me o'er,
　　Come boat me o'er to Charlie;
　　I'll gi'e John Ross anither bawbee
　　To ferry me o'er to Charlie.

　　We'll o'er the water, we'll o'er the sea,
　　We'll o'er the water to Charlie;
　　Come weal, come woe, we'll gather and go,
　　And live or die wi' Charlie."

Chapter 10

CASTLES

Castles were first built in Aberdeenshire by the Anglo-Norman settlers, who became the chief landowners when the kings of the **Canmore** line introduced feudalism. The dwelling-houses of the feudal barons were also the headquarters from which the surrounding districts were governed. Laws were enforced by the barons' officials and offenders were tried by the barons' courts. Castles thus played an important part in local government, but they were also essential links in the military organisation of the country. They were the fortified bases from which opposition to the king was quelled and, until cannons came into general use, the success of any military campaign depended upon gaining control of the castles in the area. In times of war, the local inhabitants looked to the castles for protection, and tenants, when summoned to fulfil their military service under the feudal system, gathered in the courtyard of the castles belonging to their lord, who led them into battle.

From the beginning therefore, military factors had the greatest influence on the siting and planning of castles, many of which were built to guard strategic routes such as those across the **Mounth.** When new weapons and tactics were adopted, the designs were changed accordingly and alterations and additions were made to existing buildings or completely new castles were erected. Gradually, greater provision was made for more comfortable and more spacious accommodation, but even when the need for fortified houses had passed the military origin of the castle remained obvious, since turrets and parapets were used for purposes of adornment in the later mansion-houses of country gentlemen.

Earthworks

The earliest castles were not massive stone buildings but **Mottes** or **Motte and Bailey Castles.** A motte was a flat-topped, conical, earthen mound, which was surrounded at the base by a wide, deep ditch and on the top by a strong wooden stockade, within which was the lord's wooden tower. A courtyard or bailey, which was on a lower level than the motte, was often attached to the main mound to form a motte and bailey castle. The sleeping-quarters, kitchen, chapel, stables, and other buildings required by the garrison were grouped within the palisade on top of the bailey, which was also enclosed by a ditch. A wooden ladder connected the bailey to the motte and if the former was captured the garrison withdrew to the higher level and, having taken up the ladder behind them, continued the defence of the castle.

There were many earthworks in Aberdeenshire and the sites of some of them may still be seen. On of the best examples is **The Bass of Inverurie,** where a motte and bailey castle, with the main mound over fifty feet high, was built towards the end of the twelfth century. The Peel of Strathbogie, which was erected about the same time, occupied the site overlooking the River Deveron where the ruins of the later Huntly Castle now stand. At Strathdon, the Earls of Mar had a castle on the **Doune of Invernochty,** which is over sixty feet high, measures about three quarters of an acre on top, and is crowned by a stone wall six feet thick. It is surrounded by a twenty-five feet wide ditch, which is thirty feet deep in some places and was flooded from a lake formed by damming part of the marshy ground to the north of the Doune.

Although some of the Aberdeenshire earthworks are known as **Peels,** e.g. the Peel of Fichlie near Towie and the Peel Bog of Lumphanan, this does not mean that they were crowned by the square, stone-and-lime towers of the type later known in the south of Scotland as " Border Peels." The word "peel" comes from the French "pel" which was derived from the Latin "palus" meaning " a stake." Originally therefore, a peel was a timber palisade, which was built to strengthen the defence of a timber castle, but in some cases the word came to be applied to a motte or motte and bailey with a wooden paling surmounting its earthen mound.

Motte and bailey castles were easily set on fire by attackers shooting blazing arrows into them. As a defence against this, the timberwork was sometimes daubed with clay, but it was only when stone and lime were used in their construction that castles became safe from attack by fire. Although the first stone castles were built in the County during the thirteenth century, many of the earthworks, such as Invernochty, Fichlie, and Strathbogie, continued to be used until the fifteenth century.

Enclosure-Type Castles

The simplest type of stone castle consisted of a high wall enclosing a courtyard, within which were the wooden buildings of the garrison. Such a castle once stood at King Edward.

It was usual, however, for large round towers to be built at the corners of the walls. The biggest tower was commonly furthest from the gate and contained its own water-supply in the form of an underground well. It was known as the **Donjon** or **Keep** and could be defended even if the remainder of the castle was captured. The buildings within the enclosure, such as the hall, the kitchen, and the solar or lord's residence, were usually grouped along the wall furthest from the entrance, which was always the weakest part of a castle. During the thirteenth century, enclosure-type castles were built at Coull, Migvie, and Kildrummy.

The first of these, which is thought to have been destroyed by Robert Bruce to prevent it being used by the English, had six round towers and a massive wall enclosing a large courtyard. It was erected by the Durwards as the principal stronghold on their estates, which stretched from Coull to Skene, and from Alford to Invercanny. It was not so big, however, as Kildrummy, which was at one time the most important castle in Aberdeenshire and, although in ruins, is still the most complete example of an enclosure-type castle in Scotland.

The building of Kildrummy Castle to guard part of the route into Moray, which was still proving troublesome to the Scottish kings, was commenced during the reign of Alexander II. (See Chapter 4.) It played a big part in Scottish history, being visited by Edward I of England in 1296 and 1303; captured by the English after Osbarn's betrayal in 1306; and successfully defended by John of the Craig in 1335. (See Chapter 5.) It was garrisoned by Royalists and then captured by Cromwell's troops in 1654. (See Chapter 8.) Less than forty years later, it was burned by the Jacobite troops of Bonnie Dundee to prevent it being used by the supporters of William III and, having been partly repaired, was the base from which the Earl of Mar planned the 1715 Jacobite Rebellion, after which it was finally dismantled by Government troops. (See Chapter 9.)

The five-sided courtyard at Kildrummy was enclosed by a massive wall with four large towers. Along the north side, which is furthest from the gate and overlooks a deep ravine, were ranged the solar, the hall and the kitchen, between the two round towers, namely the Snow Tower and the Warden's Tower. The Snow Tower, which was over one hundred feet high and had five stone-vaulted storeys, was the keep, with its own water-supply from a deep underground well. At the opposite side of the courtyard, the main entrance was guarded by a huge gatehouse, which was erected on the orders of Edward I when his troops occupied the castle during the Wars of Independence.

Tower Houses

As a result of the impoverished state of the country during, and for many years after, the Wars of Independence, no more enclosure-type castles were built. The few castles which were constructed during the fourteenth century were Tower houses, which were the cheapest possible fortified dwelling-houses. The typical tower was rectangular, with very thick stone walls, and contained one vaulted room on each storey. The kitchen was in the basement and the living accommodation above, with a spiral stair connecting the rooms. To give extra security, the door was at first floor level and was reached by a wooden ladder, which could be drawn up if the castle was attacked. There were few or no openings on the ground floor and the defence was conducted from loop-holes in the upper storeys and from the roof parapet. The fortifications were usually strengthened by the addition of a barmekin or small courtyard enclosed by a stone wall.

The tower of the present Drum Castle was originally a tower house and is thought to have been built towards the end of the thirteenth century. About seventy feet high, with walls twelve feet thick at the basement, it contained three vaulted storeys surmounted by a cap-house and parapet. The cap-house has been replaced by a flat roof in the modern building, but the parapet has remained unaltered since the castle came into the hands of the

Irvine family in 1323. (See Chapter 5.) Entry to the tower is gained by a door on the first floor which is now reached by a stone stair instead of a wooden ladder.

L-plan Castles

A rectangular tower, with a first floor entrance and only one room on each storey was not a very suitable dwelling-house and, by the fifteenth century, the master-masons had introduced a new type of tower house which was L-shaped. By adding a wing at right angles to the long side of the main building, they not only provided extra accommodation but also made it possible to have the door on the ground floor, in the easily defended angle between the two wings.

L-plan castles were built at Fedderate and Ravenscraig near Peterhead towards the end of the fifteenth century. The plan remained popular and many L-shaped tower houses were erected in Aberdeenshire during the sixteenth and seventeenth centuries.

Two-stepped or Link-planned Castles

Until fire-arms came into general use in the sixteenth century, the defence of a tower house was conducted mainly from the roof-top, where the archers could shelter behind the high parts of the parapet after firing from the low parts. It was quite common to have a corbelled parapet, with spaces between every second support so that boiling water, molten lead, stones, and other heavy objects could be thrown down on the attackers. In the sixteenth century, however, changes had to be made to allow defenders to use hand guns to the best advantage. This meant that the L-plan was altered slightly and the wing was replaced by a square or round tower, which was built diagonally from the main block to form a link-planned or two-stepped castle. Loop-holes were provided on the ground floor, from which the defence was now mainly conducted. Link-planned castles were erected at Pitfichie, in the sixteenth century, and at Birse near Aboyne in the seventeenth century.

Z-plan Castles

The next development in the plan of the tower house was the addition of square or round towers at two diagonally opposite corners of the main building. With this arrangement, the men in the towers could cover all sides of the main block, the occupants of which could in turn cover the towers. Extra accommodation was also available and no part of the castle overshadowed any other, an important point when windows were very small and the amount of light reaching the interior limited. A big proportion of the Z-plan castles in Scotland was built in the north-east, especially in the Alford and Garioch districts, where good examples may be seen at Glenbuchat, Midmar, Harthill, and Pitcaple.

Better Accommodation and The Palace Plan

The additions and alterations which were made to the basic tower-house plan had been the result mainly of defensive considerations. From the later years of the sixteenth century onwards, however, greater attention was paid to the standard of accommodation within the castles and also to their outward appearance. Even when the traditional designs were used, as in the L-planned Craigievar Castle in 1626 and in the Z-planned buildings of Midmar in the latter part of the sixteenth century and Castle Fraser in 1617, the emphasis was no longer on the military side of the castle. This desire to provide better living-quarters is also evident at Drum, where the additions which were made to the tower in 1619 now form the south wing of the castle, as well as at Keith Hall, where the original Z-plan building was incorporated in the mansion-house erected by the first Earl of Kintore in the second half of the seventeenth century.

The move towards more spacious accommodation gave rise to the further development of the "palace" plan, the earliest and simplest example of which had been built at Kindrochit before 1371. A large hall now displaced the keep as the most important part of the castle, which consisted of a quadrangular set of buildings around a central courtyard. Between 1584 and 1589, additions were made to the Auld Tower at Tolquhon to form a castle of this type, and in the sixteenth and seventeenth centuries, similar alterations were made at Pitsligo.

The two finest examples of palatial castles in Aberdeenshire, however, were possibly Fvyie and Huntly. The former consisted of buildings of various periods, the oldest of which still form part of the frontal range of the present L-shaped castle, the Preston Tower having been erected at the end of the fourteenth century, the Meldrum Tower about 1440, and the Seton Tower at the end of the sixteenth century. The highly ornate crow-stepped gables, corbelling, and turrets were added during the sixteenth and seventeenth centuries, while the Gordon Tower was built in 1777. Huntly Palace was constructed between 1600 and 1604 on the site of the Peel of Strathbogie to replace the castle which was destroyed when the Roman Catholic earls rebelled against James VI. (See Chapter 7.) A French mason was employed on the building and his influence is obvious from the great row of oriel windows which is one of the main architectural features of the castle.

When the need for fortified dwelling-houses had completely passed and military factors no longer influenced designs, the mansions of County landowners continued to be based on the plans which had been developed during the previous centuries. Towers, turrets, and battlements were still included for purposes of adornment, not only when existing castles were altered, as when the Z-plan building at Cluny was incorporated in the nineteenth century castle, but also when completely new structures, such as Balmoral, were erected.

Appendix to Chapter 10

Further examples of the various types of castles:

EARTHWORKS

Education Area	Site
Aberdeen	Tillydrone, Aberdeen
Alford	Auchindoir
	Castlehill, Kildrummy
	Kinbattock
	Midmar
Deeside	Coldstone
	Hall of Logie Ruthven
	Strachan
Ellon	Moot Hill, Ellon
Huntly	Lesmoir
Peterhead	Castle Hill, Rattray
Turriff	Moathead at Kirkton of Auchterless

TOWERS

Education Area	Site	Date
Alford	Corgarff	16-17th Century
Deeside	Kindrochit	1390
Ellon	Tolquhon	1420
	Udny	16th Century
Fraserburgh	Cairnbulg	1380
	Pitsligo	15th Century
Garioch	Hallforest	Early 14th Century

L-PLAN

Education Area	Site	Date
Alford	Craig	16th Century
	Colquhoney	16th Century
	Tillycairn	Between 1548 and 1580
	Towie	1571
Deeside	Braemar	1628
Ellon	House of Schivas	About 1560
Garioch	Leslie	1661
Huntly	Drumminor	1440
Turriff	Delgaty	1570
	Gight	16th Century

LINK-PLANNED

Education Area	Site	Date
Alford	Balfluig	1556
	Corse	1581
Deeside	Abergairn	1614
	Abergeldie	Mid-16th Century

Z-PLAN

Education Area	Site	Date
Alford	Asloun	16th Century
	Terpersie	1561
Ellon	Arnage	
Fraserburgh	Cairnbulg (Additions to the Tower House.)	1545

Chapter 11

COUNTRY LIFE IN STEWART TIMES

Hamlets and Cottowns

Most of the people in Aberdeenshire during Stewart times lived in small hamlets or cottowns. In a hamlet, there were about six to twelve houses, each with a garden, or kailyard, and a stack of peats beside it. The inhabitants were mainly farm-workers, but in some hamlets there might be a miller, a tinker, a tailor, a smith, a horner, or a pewterer. The tinker was the man who mended pots and pans; the horner made spoons and other household utensils from horn; and the pewterer made jugs and plates from pewter. The tailor, who travelled about from place to place, was always a welcome visitor as he was a source of news from the surrounding countryside. When he was asked to make clothes for somebody, he lived and worked in the house belonging to his customer. There were no clothing shops at this time and it was not possible to buy ready-made clothes. Another welcome visitor to the hamlet was the chapman, who sold goods from a big pack which he carried on his back.

Each farm had its "fairm toun", or cottown, consisting of a few houses in which the cottars, or farm servants, lived. Some of the cottars had a cow, a few sheep, and a small piece of land which they farmed themselves, but most of the time they worked on the big farm.

There were no good roads, with hard, smooth surfaces, between the hamlets and cottowns. In many places there were only narrow tracks, full of deep holes, and in winter they were covered with mud and water. News travelled slowly and there was little trade between the various places. Most people did not go far from home and those who did either walked or went on horse-back. There were no proper carts or carriages. Goods were transported on sledges, or in creels or bundles slung across the backs of pack-horses, which were small and not very strong.

Buildings

No cement and little lime was used in ordinary building during Stewart times and the houses in the hamlets and cottowns were very poor. The walls were made of rough stones and divots, with the spaces between filled in with clay. The roof consisted of turf, straw, heather, or broom, laid on top of rough wooden couples, and covered with clay to keep out the water. Ropes of straw were used to tie down the roof so that it would not be blown away.

The better houses had three rooms, a **But** and **Ben,** and a small room between them. The ben, which was the best room, was only used when important people, such as the minister or the laird, visited the house. It had an earthen floor, which was usually carpeted with rushes or strewn with sand since the inhabitants could not afford to buy any floor-covering. There was no plaster, paper, or paint on the walls. In the gable-end was a wide, open fireplace, in which peats and wood were burned — very little coal was used by common country people in Stewart times. Above the fire was a **Hingin' Lum,** which looked like a wooden box, about five feet long and open at both ends. It was covered with clay and tied with straw ropes on the outside. Chimneys of this type easily caught fire and the roofs of the houses were often burned.

The room at the other end, the but, was used as a kitchen, a living-room, and a bedroom. In the fireplace, a metal rod was suspended and pivoted so that pots could be hung on it. This was known as a **Swee** or a **Sway.** Usually, there was no chimney but only a hole in the roof to allow the smoke to escape. The windows were very small and there was no glass in them. The furniture was very simple, being roughly made of wood by the people themselves or by the local joiner.

The little room between the but and the ben was sometimes known as the **Spence** and was used as a store for such things as bowls of milk and home-made ale, the meal girnal in which the oatmeal was kept, and the jar of sowens, which were made by soaking the husks of corn in water. The spence was often used as a bedroom for the younger members of the family.

At night, the house was dimly lit. Usually, the only light came from the fire, but on special occasions a fir candle or rush light was used. The fir candle was made from the root of a fir tree which had been dug out of a peat bog. It was either placed in a special holder called a "peer man" or was held by one of the young boys in the family or by a beggar who was being given shelter for the night. An old poem describes the youngest boy holding the candle as follows:

> "An' little Pate sits i' the neuk,
> An' but-a-hoose dare hardly look,
> But haud an' snuff the Fir."

The wicks for the rush lights were made of the dried inside parts of rushes which were gathered when there was a full moon, as the people believed they would give a better light if cut at this time. The wicks were placed in holders known as **Cruisies** which contained dogfish liver oil.

The barns and stables were built in the same way as the dwelling-houses. The lower part of the walls was made of rough stones and the upper part of turf. The roof was thatched with divots or heather.

The poorer dwelling-houses had no chimneys and the smoke from the peat fire, which was sometimes placed on stones in the middle of the floor, found its way out by the door or through a hole in the roof. There was no proper division into rooms. One end was occupied by the family and the other by the animals, with a thin partition about half the height of the house, between them.

Infield and Outfield

Much of the land could not be cultivated as it was covered with huge stones or was too wet because the farmers did not drain it. Farm-land was divided into two parts — Infield and Outfield — but there was no fence between them. The infield, which was usually about one fifth of the farm, was the land nearest the steading and it was cultivated every year. It was divided into three parts, oats being grown in two of them while a kind of barley, known as "bere", was grown on the third. There were no turnips, potatoes, or clover at this time. Each year, only one of the parts of the infield was given farm-manure. This scarcity of fertilizer, together with the fact that the same crops were grown year after year, led to the soil being ruined. The yield was very low and farmers were content if they grew enough for food for themselves and their animals and for seed in the following year, and had enough left to pay the rent of the farm. As an old couplet puts it:

"Ane tae saw, ane tae gnaw,
An' ane tae pay the laird witha'."

The outfield was divided into two parts — the **Folds** and the **Faughs** — each of which was sub-divided into ten. Every year, a dyke of divots was built round one of the parts of the folds and the animals were enclosed there for a short time during the day and also for the night. The dyke was erected in a different part each year until all the ten parts had been used. In this way, each of the folds received a little manure once every ten years. For the first five years after receiving the manure, oats were cultivated and then wild grass was allowed to grow for the next five years. In the faughs, which were never manured, oats were grown half the time and wild grass for the other half. The crops from both parts of the outfield were very, very poor and were often not worth the work put out on them, while the grass was full of weeds and so was not much good as feeding-stuff.

Runrig Farming

In some places, the land on a farm was shared among two or more farmers. It was divided into pieces known as **Rigs,** between which were strips or **Balks,** which were never cultivated. Each farmer was given a number of rigs in different parts of the farm so that he had some of the good land and also some of the bad land. After a time, the land was shared out again and each farmer was given different rigs. This was known as Runrig Farming and was not a good method. The land in the balks was wasted and was always covered with weeds, which spread to the rigs. It was difficult for a good farmer to make improvements if he shared a farm with a lazy man, especially when he was given different rigs after some years and so somebody else benefited from his hard work. Very often there would be only one plough for the whole farm and each farmer was supposed to provide some of the oxen to pull it. Sometimes the farmers could not afford a plough and had to borrow one from a bigger farm, where they had to work in return for the loan and so their own land was not properly looked after.

Implements

The implements used by farmers in Stewart times were of poor quality. They were made mostly of wood and so were easily broken. Wooden ploughs, costing less than ten shillings each were made by the local joiners, who could make three of them in a day. The plough was pulled by oxen and since as many as twelve were usually yoked to the implement, it was known as the **Twal Ousen Plough.** The furrows were S-shaped because it was difficult to turn the oxen at the end of the rigs without taking a wide sweep. It used to be said, however, that farmers made such furrows so that the oxen would not have to go in a straight line and would therefore be a more difficult target for the witches, who were supposed to be trying to shoot them! Harrows were made of wood with points of whin roots. The harness used with them was made of twisted rushes or straw, or of fir roots which were later used for candles. Some farmers had harness of hair from cows' tails for they thought that this would prevent witches from damaging the crops and livestock and, long after hemp and chain harness became common, a few feet of hair rope continued to be inserted next the animals for protection.

Threshing was usually done, a little at a time, in the winter mornings before it was light enough for outside work. The farm-worker spread some corn on the barn floor and beat it with a **Flail** until the ears were knocked away from the stalks. He next riddled the corn, making as much draught as possible so that the chaff was blown to one side and the ears were left lying on the floor.

The Mill

When a farmer was going to grind his corn into meal, he was supposed to use the mill belonging to the laird. The mill stood beside a stream so that the water could drive the big mill-wheel, which made the grinding-stones go round and crush the corn. The inhabitants of the cottowns and hamlets had to do all the work in building the mill and in keeping it in order as one of the many unpaid services which they had to perform for the laird. When the corn was ground, a part of it was kept as payment for the laird and also for the miller.

Payments In Kind

Little money was used when paying the rents of farms in Stewart times. Payments were made in kind, that is, in goods. For example, the rent of a farm in the high-lying parish of Tough, in the middle of the sixteenth century, was eight merks (about 8/11d.), two sheep, a dozen hens, one pig, and a quantity of peats. The rent for the same size of farm in the low-lying parish of Foveran was eight merks, one boll of malt, one and a half bolls of meal, two bolls of oats, two sheep, one dozen hens, and peats. You will notice that the payment for a low-lying farm was higher than for an upland farm and included some of the crops grown on the farm as well as livestock. On the other hand, since the crops on the higher farm were poorer, the payment was made mostly in animals.

The farm people had also to do much work for the laird without being paid for it. One of the jobs they had to do was tramping farm grain. The oats grown in Stewart times had a long black covering which had to be removed before the grinding took place. To do this, the oats were heated in a kiln and then people walked backwards and forwards over the hot oats until all the black coverings had fallen off. The farm servants had also to dig peats and carry them to the laird's house. They had to help with the ploughing, the harrowing, and the harvesting, using short, curved sickles for cutting the corn. Sometimes, they had to carry goods, in creels, from Aberdeen to the Home Farm or Mains, as the laird's farm was usually called. They also had to help to thatch the church, the manse, and the school, if there happened to be one in the neighbourhood.

Cattle Feeding

Farmers did not grow proper hay and as they had no turnips they could not feed many cattle in their byres during the winter. They used crushed whins and boiled chaff as fodder, but even then many of the cows were killed at Martinmas, in November, and the meat was salted so that it could be used during the winter. A cow which was killed and salted at Martinmas was called a "mart" and the farmer usually had to give one to the laird as part of his rent.

When spring came and the cattle which had survived the winter were being let out to the fields again, they were often so weak, due to lack of feeding, that the farm-servants had to carry them. Once outside, they were tended by the herd, who had to prevent them from straying among the crops growing in the un-enclosed fields.

As you may imagine, people in Stewart times had a very hard life. Working hours were long and there were no machines to help with the various tasks. In winter time, farm servants had to begin work at four o'clock in the morning to thresh the daily supply of corn with a flail, while in summer-time work usually began at five o'clock. In the evenings, there was little or no entertainment. There were no newspapers and most of the people could not read the "chap" books, which were sold by the chapman and usually contained poems about William Wallace and Robert Bruce. Women spent the evenings washing, dyeing, and spinning wool, while men wove cloth on a hand-loom or made harness from straw or hair. Boys and girls went to work while very young, often at the age of nine years. The former started as herd laddies and the latter as housemaids and nursemaids. Bad harvests were common and food was often scarce and dear. Foodstuffs were seldom carried long distances, so that while there might be a surplus in one part there might be a shortage in another. As we shall see in Chapter 13, it was not until the nineteenth century that changes were made which led to Aberdeenshire becoming a very good farming area, with famines a thing of the past and with the people enjoying a much higher standard of life.

Chapter 12
TOWN LIFE IN STEWART TIMES

Streets and Buildings

The towns of Aberdeenshire at the end of the sixteenth century were very small compared with those of the present day. For example, Aberdeen had less than 8,000 inhabitants — to-day it has more than 180,000; Peterhead had between 200 and 300 — to-day it has over 12,000; and Inverurie consisted of only one short street with houses scattered at both sides of it.

The main streets in Aberdeen were very narrow, had very poor surfaces, and were badly paved. They were linked by even narrower vennels, wynds, rows, and lanes, all of which were very untidy. Refuse from the houses was thrown into the streets, where it lay until swept up by the public scavenger. Disease spread quickly and there were frequent outbreaks of the plague. Leprosy was quite common, due to bad feeding and poor sanitation, and the lepers were confined to huts on the outskirts of the town. Pigs roamed about just as dogs do to-day, and searched for food in the middens, which stood behind the houses and were usually emptied once a year, when the contents were carted to the town fields to be used as manure. On special occasions, such as a Royal visit, laws were passed ordering all inhabitants to keep their pigs off the streets, to clear out the styes, and to empty the middens so that the smell would not be so bad as usual. In 1511, for example, when James IV visited the town, the people in the Ship Row, which was then the main thoroughfare, were ordered to hang sweet-smelling herbs on their houses.

Most of the houses in the towns were poorly built. In Inverurie, they were similar to the country cottages which were described in Chapter II, being made of uncemented stones and turf, with low roofs thatched with broom or heather. Many houses, which were built with their gables facing the street, had byres and barns beside them for, in addition to being tradesmen and craftsmen, the town-dwellers were farmers, each with his share of the town common and fields, which were cultivated on the runrig system. There were no shops. The craftsmen worked in their homes and their products were displayed for sale at the market stance beside the Cross on the weekly market-days.

There were some well-built stone houses in Aberdeen. **Provost Ross's House** in the Ship Row, for example, bears the date 1593, and there is evidence that the other houses in that street were equally well constructed. (The first recorded Provost of Aberdeen was Richard Cementarius or Richard the Mason, which seems to indicate that there were well-qualified masons in the town as early as the thirteenth century.) Many of the houses, however, were still built of wood or of wood and plaster and so outbreaks of fire were common. All fires had to be put out at sunset in summer and at 8 or 9 p.m. in winter, and were not supposed to be re-lit before 5 o'clock the next morning. This was known as the "curfew". (The French words "couvre feu" mean "cover fire".)

The houses of the noblemen, such as the Earl Marischal's at the Castlegate and the Earl of Mar's at the Gallowgate, consisted of a forehouse or fronthouse with a close or yard, surrounded by buildings, behind it. The forehouse usually had a wooden balcony and an outside stair at the front, and a covered passage leading through to the yard behind. The roof was covered with stone slabs instead of the thatch or divots which provided the roofs of the poorer houses. These were built gable-end on to the street and had clay or mud walls. Only the best houses had glass in the windows. The householder very often took it with him if he moved to a new house, in the same way as he took the tapestries with which the walls were covered. There were earthen floors, which, in the better houses, were carpeted with rushes mixed with sweet herbs, but were left bare or sprinkled with sand in the poorer houses.

Apart from the church, the most important building in the town was the **Tolbooth** which, in addition to being the office for the collection of tolls or taxes, was used as a jail and also as a meeting-place for the Town Council.

Burghs and Burgesses

Since the twelfth century, the practice of creating burghs had become increasingly common. There were three kinds of burghs, the most important being **Royal Burghs,** which received their charters from the king, to whom they paid a fixed amount of rent annually. The others, **Burghs of Barony** and **Burghs of Regality,** were erected under some noble or leading churchman, to whom the inhabitants had to pay dues. Some of the burghs which were established in Stewart times have long since disappeared, but others have developed into the leading towns in the County to-day.

Aberdeen, Inverurie, and Kintore had been founded as Royal Burghs before the end of the twelfth century. (See Chapter 4.) The earliest charters are no longer in existence but, in the case of Kintore, for example, tradition has it that the first charter was granted by Kenneth II, who ruled from 971 to 995. According to the story, the inhabitants of the village helped the king to defeat a Danish army by driving their cattle, covered with oak branches, through the enemy position and Kenneth, in gratitude, created Kintore a Royal Burgh. Fyvie was a Royal Burgh from before the fourteenth century, the site being at Woodhead, where a Tolbooth and Market Cross were in existence in the eighteenth century, while Rattray became a Royal Burgh in the time of Mary, Queen of Scots.

Burghs of Barony were established at Old Rayne and Kildrummy in the fourteenth century, at Clatt in 1501, at Turriff in 1511, at Huntly in 1545, and at Insch in 1566. Peterhead became a Burgh of Barony as a result of a bargain between James IV and Robert Keith, the Commendator of the Abbey of Deer, in 1587. Four years later, Fraserburgh, which was established on the site of the old burgh of Faithlie by Sir Alexander **Fraser of Philorth,** became a Burgh of Regality.

Although the word "burgh" means "a fortified place", none of the towns in the County were enclosed by a wall. Aberdeen, however, had gates at the six main entrances to the town. These were closed at night and guarded by the watch, which patrolled the streets. The inhabitants, by living together, were better prepared to resist attack but, as was the case elsewhere in Scotland, the main reason for creating burghs was to encourage trade and the privileges granted in the foundation charters aimed at doing this.

By the terms of one of its charters, Aberdeen was allowed to have a weekly market and an annual fair, which lasted for fourteen days. As a Royal Burgh, it had wide privileges of trade in the County and also had a monopoly of foreign trade. Fraserburgh, as well as having two weekly markets was granted two annual fairs, each of which lasted for eight days, while Turriff and Insch each had one weekly market and two annual fairs.

Burgesses had to perform certain duties in return for their privileges. They had to arm themselves and be ready to defend the town; they had to "watch and ward"; and as vassals of the king or a baron, they had to be ready to follow him to war. To accustom them to the use of their weapons, wapinschaws, or weapon shows, were held periodically and anyone who was absent was fined. At Inverurie, burgesses had to help in repairing the roads leading to the peat moss and the ford across the River Don, and also give assistance in building the walls of the cattle folds and the dam dyke at the burgh mill. At Peterhead, in return for the right of casting peats in the Burgh Moss, grazing their cattle on the Burgh Common, taking part in trade, and using one boat for white fishing, the citizens had to do personal service to their superior, the Earl Marischal, and undertake to build a stone, slated house for themselves within seven years of being given their feu. At Fraserburgh, the burgesses were granted the privilege of landing their fishing boats and gathering bait on the sea-shore.

The baron was empowered to choose the bailies and other town officials in a Burgh of Barony, and in a Royal Burgh, the king had the same powers. In time, however, the king allowed the burgesses to elect the Town Council. Before a man could become a burgess, he had to own land in the burgh, pay a fee of 13/4d. Scots to the burgh funds, and take the **Burgess Oath.** The **Provost** and **Bailies** had to make the laws for the town, punish offenders, collect taxes, organise the defences in time of war, and regulate fairs and markets. Strict laws compelled all merchants to buy and sell goods in the burghs and nowhere else, and guilds were formed to ensure that the regulations were obeyed.

Merchant and Craft Guilds

As long as the amount of trade was small, there was no distinction between merchants and craftsmen. For example, one man might be a cloth merchant and a tailor, while another might be a leather merchant and a butcher. When, however, trade increased and more money was required to carry it on, the wealthier burgesses became merchants only and formed the Merchant Guild, while the poorer confined their activities to the crafts and formed Craft Guilds.

Only members of the Merchant Guild could take part in trade. To become a **Burgess of Guild,** a man had to undertake to give up all connection with the crafts, pay 40/- Scots to the Town Council, and provide a banquet for the guildsmen. The Merchant Guild was strictly controlled by the Town Council, which it assisted by regulating trade within the town. Officials were appointed to supervise the fairs and markets and make sure that all business was done in accordance with the laws laid down by the magistrates. Prices, weights, and measures were checked. Wine-tasters, examiners of meat, and measurers of cloth went about the stalls to prevent anyone selling merchandise which was not up to standard. The Guild also enforced the rules forbidding any business to be done before the bell was rung to signal the start of the fair.

The main Craft Guilds in Aberdeen were the Butchers, Weavers, Shoemakers, Tailors, Hammermen, and Bakers. Nobody was allowed to carry on any craft unless he was a member of the appropriate Craft Guild. After serving an apprenticeship of three or more years, an applicant for membership had to submit his "Maister-stick", or master-piece, to show that he was fully qualified in his craft. For example, an armourer had to make a sword and rapier, while a shoemaker had to make a pair of boots which would be a perfect fit for the customer. Having passed this test, the applicant had then to appear in armour before the Provost, pay his fee to the burgh funds, and take the Burgess Oath, swearing among other things, to help in the defence of the town. (Craftsmen fought at Harlaw in 1411 and at Justice Mills in 1644.) He had also to promise to keep some kind of weapon in his workshop and be ready to help to maintain public order since there were no policemen to do so. The admission ceremony was completed with a Guild Dinner after the new burgess had taken the Craft Oath and paid his dues to the Craft Fund.

Each Craft Guild appointed officials, headed by the **Deacon,** to control its own affairs, such as the length of the working day, wages, prices to be charged for articles produced, the number of apprentices each master craftsman could employ, and the maintenance of standards of workmanship. No craftsman was allowed to buy materials independently, but had to do so through the guild. For example, the Deacon of the Bakers bought wheat for all the guildsmen and so they all had to pay the same price. Every Saturday, the Deacon and officials of the Shoemakers watched the main roads into Aberdeen to ensure that all the hides which were brought into town were sold to all their members at the same price. One of the main aims of the guild system was obviously to prevent competition and to discourage individual enterprise.

In addition to controlling conditions of work, the officers of the Craft Guilds regulated the daily lives of the craftsmen, their families, and their servants. For example, they laid down rules about compulsory church attendance and suitable dress for members, dealt with cases of drunkenness and disorderliness, and punished anyone who broke the Admission Oath by expelling him from the guild and forbidding any member to speak to him or his family. The Craft Guilds also looked after sick members, helped any craftsman's widow who was in need of money, and played a big part in providing public entertainment.

Amusements

When few towns existed there was little organised public entertainment apart from that given by the acrobats, jugglers, clowns, and musicians who appeared at the fairs. To begin with, the clergy tried to stop these performances, but when they failed they themselves presented plays based on legends and Bible stories. These **Morality** and **Miracle Plays** were intended to teach the great truths of Christianity and were first acted in churches and monasteries. In time, the clergy ceased to take part in the performances, which were then given by the people themselves in the open-air since there were no theatres.

In Aberdeen, the plays were given as part of the celebrations on certain Saints' Days and holidays, such as St. Nicholas Day and May Day. They were under the control of two young citizens known as the **Abbot and Prior of Bon-Accord**. The festivities commenced at the Playfield at Woolmanhill, where the citizens assembled in their gayest clothes and then went in procession through the town before taking part in dancing, exhibitions of games, and plays. At the end of the day, the Abbot and Prior provided a magnificent banquet for those taking part.

By the beginning of the sixteenth century, the two leaders of the pageants were known as **Robin Hood** and **Little John** and they and their attendants wore green clothes and carried yellow bows and brass arrows. By that time also, the Craft Guilds were taking part in the celebrations on special festival days. They marched in procession carrying banners and emblems of their patron saints and then gave a performance of a Miracle or Morality Play, with each Craft Guild being responsible for a part of it by supplying so many actors and any necessary equipment.

These pageants were dying out before the Reformation and after that the Church prohibited them, and so when James VI decided to encourage the performance of plays in 1601, he had to ask Queen Elizabeth to send her company of actors from England. They presented several plays in Aberdeen and one account says that William Shakespeare then acted in the town, but there is no definite evidence of this.

Aberdeen had a band of minstrels, who played instruments such as the pipe, the fiddle, the trumpet, and small drums. They performed favourite pieces of music as they proceeded through the town in the early morning and at night after the ringing of the curfew bell. They also took part in all celebrations conducted by the Abbot and Prior of Bon-Accord and by Robin Hood and

Little John. At the end of the sixteenth century, the minstrels were paid two shillings a year by each of the lower class citizens, while the upper classes provided them with food and drink.

The burgesses were expected to help in amusing themselves by practising archery on Saturdays, so that they would be able to use the bow and arrow if required. Many of them, however, did not do so and laws were passed for the punishment of those who preferred to play bowls, golf, and football, all of which differed from the games we have to-day.

Education

John Knox, in the First Book of Discipline in 1561, outlined a national system of education. He suggested that there should be small rural schools with the pupils taught by the ministers of the country parishes; larger schools under schoolmasters for the bigger villages and small towns; high schools for the big towns; and universities. Lack of money, however, made it impossible for his ideas to be put into practice and many years passed before even elementary schools were established in all parts of the country.

In the early years of the seventeenth century, few children went to school and the arrangements for education in Aberdeenshire varied from area to area. For example, in the Presbytery of Ellon in 1617, there was only one schoolmaster who taught in Methlick. Even at the end of the eighteenth century, about half of the parishes in Buchan had no schooolmaster.

The more prosperous burghs, however, made better provision for education. In 1601, Kintore, Fraserburgh, and Peterhead each had a schoolmaster, while Inverurie had a grammar school by 1607. Old Aberdeen and New Aberdeen each had a university as well as a grammar school, which in the latter case dated from the middle of the thirteenth century.

In Old Aberdeen, **King's College,** which was named in honour of James IV, was founded by **Bishop William Elphinstone.** In 1494, he obtained a Bull from Pope Alexander VI allowing him to establish a college for the teaching of theology and law. By 1505, the building of the chapel was finished and students were in attendance, with **Hector Boece** as first Principal.

About a century later, in 1593, the **Earl Marischal** founded and endowed **Marischal College** in New Aberdeen, using for the purpose part of the wealth which he had confiscated from the Church. The College used the buildings of the old **Franciscan Monastery** in Broad Street until they were burned in 1639. (Both Colleges received many additions and alterations before being combined as the **University of Aberdeen** in 1860.)

For a short time, there was a third university in Aberdeenshire. In 1593, Sir Alexander Fraser of Philorth obtained royal permission to establish a university in Fraserburgh. Parliament confirmed this in 1597 and ordered that, in addition to George Ferme who was a minister in Fraserburgh, the ministers from Tyrie, Philorth, Crimond, and Rathen should act as teachers. This university is still commemorated in Fraserburgh by the street,

College Bounds, but apart from the period between 1600 and 1605, and again in 1647, when the students from King's College moved to Fraserburgh because of the plague in Aberdeen, it is doubtful if any teaching was done. Indeed, it is unlikely that the buildings were ever completed although part of them still stood in 1793.

Dress

The Scottish Parliament passed laws regulating the dress of the people by limiting the amount of money which could be spent on clothes made from imported cloth. This was an attempt to encourage home weaving. The laws seem to have been disobeyed in Aberdeen, however, for the wealthier classes usually dressed in brightly coloured clothes of velvet, silk, taffeta, and fur. The common people wore coarse woollen cloth or knitted worsteds, which were usually black or brown.

The wife of a wealthy burgess might wear a mutch covered by a red hood, a kirtle or short skirt on top of a longer skirt, which was worn over a farthingale or hooped petticoat, and a ruff of starched linen or folds of lace. The wife of an ordinary citizen commonly wore a russet gown without the farthingale and had no red hood. Brooches, lockets, and rings were worn by most women, but necklaces and ear-rings were worn only by the upper classes.

The wealthy merchant might wear a conical hat with a decorated band, or a velvet bonnet with a gold tassel, a cloak of fine silk with satin lining and silver clasps imported from France or Spain, a doublet or short tunic, with silver buttons right to the neck, made of brightly coloured silk and brocade imported from Lyons, breeches tied at the knees with taffeta garters, and stockings of cloth or worsted. At his neck, he would have a frilled ruff or big linen collar, and on his feet, boots or shoes made from fine Spanish leather. The ordinary craftsman wore a worsted shirt, a plain doublet, long stockings, and a cloak. His shoes were usually of untanned leather, with the hide side out, and long pointed toes, the length of which was restricted by law to discourage the fashion of having the toes curled several inches into the air.

Food

The ordinary townspeople depended on various forms of oatmeal, such as brose, porridge, oatcakes, and sowens, as their staple diet. To this was added an occasional dish of kale and, on rare occasions only, meat. They had no potatoes, turnips, wheat loaves, tea, or sugar. Home-brewed ale was their main drink and wild honey the usual form of sweetening. They produced most of their food themselves and were therefore affected by local shortages. When this happened, the Town Council attempted to buy oatmeal in bulk for the whole town, giving another illustration of the lack of individual action, which was one of the main features of town life in Stewart times. It was only when the Industrial Revolution had taken place that wide differences developed between town and country life and the Craft system, based on group action, was displaced by individual enterprise.

Chapter 13

THE AGRICULTURAL REVOLUTION

At the beginning of the eighteenth century, farming in Aberdeenshire was still carried on in the same way as it had been for the previous few centuries. (See Chapter II.) Implements were poor; land was not properly drained or manured; weeds grew in large numbers; huge stones were scattered over a great deal of the land, most of which was unenclosed; in several places, the run-rig system was still in use; and farmers followed the infield and outfield method of cultivation, knowing nothing about the proper rotation of crops.

Obviously there was room for improvement, but most of the ordinary farmers did not have enough money, nor did they have the desire, to make any change. All they wanted to do was to carry on in the old way without trying out anything new. During the eighteenth century, however, changes which led to better farming were made in several places in the County by some of the owners of large estates.

Some Early Improvers

One of the first to improve farming in Aberdeenshire was an English woman, the wife of the Duke of Gordon, who introduced English ploughs and ploughmen to her husband's estates in 1706. She showed the tenants that these ploughs were much better than the old twal ousen ploughs. She also demonstrated how better hay could be made from grass grown from good seeds. Most of the tenants carried on in the usual way, however, making hay from wild grass and rushes, and adding to their meagre supply of feeding stuffs by using dried thistles and crushed whins. It was not until about 1750 that some shops in Aberdeen began to sell grass seeds, and even then few farmers bought them.

The best-known improver in the north-east during the eighteenth century was **Sir Archibald Grant of Monymusk.** He made good roads on his estates and to shelter the fields which he enclosed, planted about fifty million trees, a few of which may still be seen at Old Paradise. He introduced the growing of clover, ryegrass, and turnips, in small quantities, for feeding cows, and he also tried out new crop rotations. Sir Archibald wrote a small pamphlet explaining to his tenants how they could be better farmers and offered them money to help in making improvements in their land and implements.

Another well-known improver was **Joseph Cumine of Auchry,** the founder of the village of **Cuminestown,** where he established the manufacture of linen. He planted many trees, enclosed fields, and paid special attention to the breeding of better cattle.

About the middle of the eighteenth century, **Thomas Burnett of Kenmay** and **Charles Hacket of Inveramsay** tried to encourage their tenants to be better farmers. The former is said to have been the first to grow whole fields of turnips in Aberdeenshire, while the latter was one of the first to use a seed drill for sowing seeds in straight lines so that the weeds could be more easily kept down.

Some years later, **Miss Fraser of Inverallochy** set about enclosing the fields on her farm. This practice of enclosing was becoming more common for, in 1786, an Aberdeen bookseller had the following lines as part of an advertisement:

" Songs, Bibles, Psalm-books, and the like,
As mony as would big a dyke."

Miss Fraser sowed a mixture of grass and barley seeds so that once the barley had been harvested the grass would come up free from weeds the following year. She also grew turnips for cattle feeding.

Among other farming improvers in the County during the eighteenth century were General Gordon of Fyvie, Mr. Udny of Udny, James Farquharson of Invercauld, Provost Robertson of Aberdeen, Sir William Forbes of Pitsligo, and the Earl of Aboyne, who is said to have built forty miles of stone dykes.

Three "Improving" Societies

The changes which were being made in Aberdeenshire had all been tried out in the south of Scotland, especially in the Lothians, and in England. To help farmers all over Scotland to learn about the new methods, and to encourage more improvements, the **Society of Improvers in the Knowledge of Agriculture in Scotland** was formed in Edinburgh in 1723, with twenty-nine men from Aberdeenshire among its members. Although they did all they could to bring about improvements, few followed their example. In 1730, **A Small Society of Farmers in Buchan** was formed. In spite of the fact that its members said that they wished to improve farming, all they did was to tell farmers to continue doing things in the old way. In 1784, the **Highland Society,** known to-day as **The Royal Highland and Agricultural Society of Scotland,** was formed in Edinburgh. It encouraged better farming by giving grants of money to farmers who grew clover and ryegrass, but it was several years before these crops became common in the County.

New Crop Rotations

About the middle of the eighteenth century, some Aberdeenshire farmers began to use lime as fertiliser. It was dear and, because of the bad roads, difficult to transport from the quarry to the farm. Moreover, there were no carts in many parts of the County and the lime had to be carried in creels or baskets. As a result, only a small quantity of it was used, but it did help to grow better crops.

The introduction of liming and the growing of clover, ryegrass, and turnips led to the infield and outfield system being done away with in several places in the County. Changes were made in the three-year crop rotation of oats, oats, barley, and then back to oats again. With the introduction of sown grasses, some farmers began to use a seven-year rotation, growing the following crops: peas in the first year; barley in the second year; grass in the third, fourth, and fifth years; oats in the sixth and seventh years; and then back to peas again. Later, when turnips were being grown as a field crop, an eight-year rotation was introduced. Turnips, well-manured, were grown in the first year; barley in the second year; grass in the third, fourth, and fifth years; oats in the sixth, seventh, and eighth years; and then turnips again.

Cattle Breeding

For centuries, it had been usual for cattle to be used for pulling farm implements before being killed for beef. This practice was continued for most of the eighteenth century and, as late as 1790, one third of all the cattle in Aberdeenshire were kept as working animals.

There were two Aberdeenshire breeds of cattle. The first, the **Buchan Humlies,** were black and hornless. They were small and not very strong, and only the poorest farmers used them for ploughing. The other breed had long horns and, being bigger and stronger than the humlies, made good working animals, which were also suitable for beef.

Towards the end of the eighteenth century, both breeds were greatly improved as a result of the increasing use of hay and turnips for winter feeding. Between 1780 and 1810, the average size of the cattle in the County was doubled, and from then on Aberdeenshire gradually became the best cattle-producing area in Scotland.

In addition to the improvement resulting from the increasing use of turnips, three other factors led to a rise in the price of cattle and encouraged Aberdeenshire farmers to become breeders. Britain was at war and there was a big demand for salt meat for the armed forces. The farmers in the Lothians had begun to pay more attention to crop-growing than to cattle-breeding and so fewer cows were being sent to the big sales at Crieff and Falkirk. English cattle-dealers bought cattle in Scottish markets from about 1776 and this also led to a bigger demand for cows.

Cattle Markets

During the seventeenth century, there were regular cattle markets at such places as Inverurie, Turriff, Rayne, and Old Deer. For many years, however, only a few cattle were sold at these markets and it was not until the second half of the eighteenth century that the cattle trade was greatly increased at the various Aberdeenshire fairs.

A fair was more than a place for buying and selling. Jugglers, acrobats, musicians, and actors all came to the fair, which was looked on as a place of amusement by the local people, who sometimes brought home-made articles, such as stockings and cloth, to sell there. Pedlars also came to the fair to sell the goods which they carried in their packs.

There is a legend which tells of how one of these pedlars started the fair at Aikey Brae near Old Deer. Auld Aikey, as he was called, was crossing the River Ugie on stepping stones when he slipped and let his pack fall into the water. It was a sunny day and he spread out his goods to dry. Many people passed and some of them bought the various articles until, by the end of the day, Aikey's pack was empty. He told his customers that he would return to the same spot on the same day the following year, when they could buy goods from him again. He did this, taking other pedlars with him, and so **Aikey Fair** is said to have begun. Each year, more and more people came to buy and sell and, by the end of the eighteenth century, Aikey was the biggest fair in the north of Scotland, as many as six thousand cattle being sold there every year.

There were no salesmen or auctioneers at the fairs. All business was done by private bargain; that is, the farmer who was selling the cow agreed on a price with the man who wished to buy it.

Cattle Droving

During the late spring and early summer, cattle dealers were busy at the fairs, buying cows and gathering them together into big herds, or **Droves,** so that they could be sent off in time for the autumn **Trysts** at **Crieff** and **Falkirk.** Trysts were big markets at which buyers and sellers had agreed to meet at certain times each year to do business. The men who brought the droves to the trysts were known as **Drovers.** They were well armed with swords and pistols to protect the cattle against robbers, such as the famous Rob Roy. (It is interesting to note that the Black Watch regiment was begun as a guard against cattle thieves.)

The leader of the drovers, known as the **Topsman,** had to plan the route and also arrange stopping-places for the drove each night. The cattle were not herded along very quickly, going only about ten miles daily. The topsman tried to keep the drove clear of the main roads and towns, and followed routes which, used year after year by thousands of cattle, came to be called **Drove Roads.** They were not specially made roads with hard surfaces, such as we have to-day, but were, as far as possible, grass-covered tracks leading through the valleys between the hills and mountains and lying beside the rivers and lochs, so that the cattle would have plenty to drink.

Sometimes, however, the cows had to travel over hard ground and many of them became lame. To prevent their hooves from being too badly damaged, they were shod with metal plates. When being shod, a cow might be injured for it was turned on its back and its legs were tied together. Then, while its head was held down by two men, the shoes were nailed on by a blacksmith, or by one of the drovers who carried a bundle of spare shoes.

During the night, the droves were allowed to stay, free of charge, in special stopping-places known as **Stances.** For example, droves which came through Corgarff stopped at West Tornahaish;

for those which crossed from the headwaters of the River Don to Braemar there were stances at Inchrory and Loch Builg; and for droves passing through the Garioch there was a stopping-place at the foot of Bennachie.

There were few bridges across the rivers in Aberdeenshire in the eighteenth century — for example, there were only four across the River Dee — and a toll, or money payment, was charged for all the traffic which used them. The drovers therefore crossed the rivers at fords, or at points where the cattle could swim, and all drove roads led to such places. Once across the River Dee, the droves continued southwards by one or other of the Mounth passes and so on to Crieff or Falkirk.

The Old with The New

Although a start had been made with improvements, changes took place very slowly and Aberdeenshire was still a backward farming area at the end of the eighteenth century. Apart from the estates of the improving lairds, most of the land was still badly cultivated, in the old-fashioned way, with poor wooden implements.

Turnips and sown grasses were rare in many parts of the County. For example, in 1795, only ten acres of turnips and forty acres of sown grass were grown in the whole Parish of Rhynie. In the Alford district also, a very small acreage of these crops was grown. Potatoes were cultivated there only in small patches, and most of the fields were not enclosed. Only a few Aberdeenshire farmers had begun to use horses for harrowing and carting, most of the work being done by oxen. The carts were small with solid wooden wheels, and could not carry heavy loads. In New Deer there were only four carts; in the whole parish of Methlick there was only one; and in Corgarff there was none, creels being used for carrying goods from place to place. In Strathdon, farmers still had to do unpaid work for the laird and so their own land was often neglected. At Fraserburgh, whole fields of turnips and potatoes were being grown and fields near the town were enclosed, but some farms were still run on the infield and outfield system. In the Cairnie district, few changes had been made and farming was in a very poor state, but at Huntly a start had been made in encouraging improvements by giving longer leases. Some farmers there had begun to drain the marshy places, but the wooden twal ousen plough was still in use, just as it was in Cromar and the Garioch.

THE NINETEENTH CENTURY

The rate at which improvements were made in farming was greatly increased during the first half of the nineteenth century. Much of the land was properly drained and enclosed. Better implements, many of them made of metal instead of wood, were used for all the jobs on the farm. Clover, ryegrass, turnips, and potatoes were grown in much larger quantities and several new fertilizers were introduced. Farms were no longer divided into infield and outfield and the runrig system was done away with.

Longer and better leases were given to tenants, most of whom adopted better crop rotations. In many places, Agricultural Clubs and Societies were formed to encourage improvements. Aberdeenshire became famous for two breeds of cattle, the Aberdeen-Angus and the Shorthorn, and instead of sending lean cattle south in droves to the trysts, farmers began to breed fat cattle which were sent south by boat, or later by railway, to markets as far away as London.

Reclaiming and Enclosing

One of the biggest improvements which took place in farming during the nineteenth century was the reclaiming and enclosing of land. Stones were cleared off the land, which was then drained, enclosed, manured, and cultivated. Most of the work was done by tenant-farmers between 1810 and 1875, and in that time the area being farmed in Aberdeenshire was more than doubled.

Some farmers, especially those near Aberdeen, sold the stones which they cleared off the fields to help to pay the expense of reclaiming. Most of the stones, however, were used locally to build dykes and steadings. Stones which were not required for this purpose were heaped into piles in the corners of fields, or into very big dykes, known as **Consumption Dykes**, such as were built at Kingswells and Glassel. We may still see the one at Kingswells, about five hundred yards long, thirty feet wide, and seven feet high.

Reclaiming was carried on all over the County but in some places more than in others. In Drumoak, for example, the whole moss of Belscavie was brought into cultivation. At Echt, the land along the Gormack burn was drained, as was the land at Cullerlie. Most of the fields on the outskirts of Aberdeen, at Pitfodels and Bucksburn, were cleared of stones and enclosed. At Kintore, between 1835 and 1875, a thousand acres were drained and enclosed, while about the same amount was reclaimed at Strichen and Methlick. From 1860, work went on at the Loch of Auchlossan near Lumphanan until 250 acres had been drained and brought into cultivation. On the other hand, little reclaiming was done at Crimond or Bennachie, where most of the farms were still in a bad state in 1875.

Implements

During the eighteenth century, better farm implements were introduced in the south of Scotland, but few of these were seen in Aberdeenshire until the early years of the nineteenth century.

In the 1760's the horse-drawn swing plough was invented by a Berwickshire farmer named **James Small.** At first, it was not used much in Aberdeenshire because farm servants were not accustomed to handling horses for ploughing and the blacksmiths, instead of copying Small's plough, continued to make ploughs of the twal ousen type. At the beginning of the nineteenth century, however, great changes were made. The swing plough became common in the County and, by about 1820, most of the ploughing was done by horses. In the second half of the century, Aberdeen-shire blacksmiths, such as Buchan of Balquhain, Newlands of Inverurie, Sellar of Huntly, and Pirie of Kinmundy, became famous for making ploughs. In 1869, Pirie made a double-farrow plough to be drawn by three horses. After being displayed at the Highland Show, it was given satisfactory public trials at the farms of Conglass and Bogend in the Garioch, and at Auchterellon. This was indeed a big change from a hundred years before, when most Aberdeenshire farmers used poor wooden implements made by the village joiner.

At the opening of the nineteenth century, harvesting was done with the sickle, but gradually the scythe replaced it. In 1808, **Mr. Gordon of Cairnbulg,** while on a visit to the south of England, saw scythes being used to cut corn. In the same year, much to the amusement of other farmers, he introduced scythes to Buchan when he cut a field of oats on the **Home Farm of Cortes** near Fraserburgh. His neighbours soon saw that the scythe was better than the sickle and they also began to use it. **William Anderson of Hatton of Fintray** introduced the scythe to that district in 1810. From then on, it was quickly adopted for cutting oats in all parts of the County, but for several years later, the sickle was used for cutting barley.

Much of the shearing with the sickle had been done by women but, when the scythe was introduced, the best men on the farm took over the cutting. In addition to the men with the scythes, women were needed to gather the corn and make bands, by plaiting straw, with which men bound the sheaves. A man was also required to draw a rake to gather the loose stalks of corn.

In 1826, **Patrick Bell,** a minister in Forfarshire, invented a reaping machine, but it was not until the 1870's that reapers began to replace scythes on the larger Aberdeenshire farms. To begin with, a man had to walk behind the reaper and lift off the corn as it was cut. Later machines threw the corn clear of the cutting blades, but it then had to be gathered and tied by hand.

In 1851, the binder, which could make sheaves as well as cut corn, was invented in America. It was first used in Scotland about 1873. At that time, the sheaves were tied with wire, but by about 1879 binders which tied with twine were in use. These were intro-duced to Aberdeenshire about 1885.

For hundreds of years, threshing had been done with the flail and winnowing with the riddle. (See Chapter II.) In 1784, **Andrew Meikle** of Dunbar invented a threshing mill and although at least one of these machines was in use in Aberdeenshire in 1791, at Auchterless, threshing with the flail was the usual method all over the County at the beginning of the nineteenth century, and continued to be so on the smaller farms for the next hundred years. On the bigger farms, however, machines were introduced for both threshing and winnowing.

On farms beside a river or stream, where there was a suitable supply of water, the mills were driven by a big water-wheel. Mills of this type were common in all parts of the County. The Bothy Ballad, "Drumdelgie", tells us:

> "At sax o'clock the mill's put on,
> To gi'e us a' strait wark;
> It tak's four o' us to mak' to her
> Till ye could wring our sark.

> And then the water is put off,
> We hurry doon the stair,
> To get some quarters through the fan
> Till daylight does appear."

In places where there was not a suitable water supply, the mills were driven by horses, which had to walk round and round in a circle all the time, turning a wheel which made the mill work.

Some of the richer farmers built mills which were driven by steam, supplied from a big boiler. The farm of Shethin in Tarves had one of these as early as the 1830's. For a time, such mills were quite common on the bigger farms in the County. Of course, they were not in use all the time, and the boilers rusted and became dangerous, so much so that a few of them exploded, injuring some farm-workers.

Gradually, fixed steam mills went out of use and were replaced by portable ones. The threshing mills and the engines for driving them were pulled from farm to farm by horses. Later, these were replaced by mills pulled and driven by traction engines.

Fertilizers and Crop Rotations

The infield and outfield system of manuring was done away with. More use was made of farm-yard manure and many new fertilizers were introduced. Farmers near the coast used sea-weed, whale blubber, and rotten fish. At St. Fergus, a short canal was built so that shelly sand, which was scattered as fertilizer, could be easily transported. In most parts of the County, lime was used in large quantities. Some of it came to Aberdeen by boat and was then carted to places as far inland as Alford. A big lime-works was opened at Ardonald in Cairnie and another at Auchairn. Farmers in Maud, Brucklay, and Whitehill carted lime from Annochie. In other places, Strathdon for example, the farmers themselves burned the lime in kilns and then spread it. Powdered bone was another new fertilizer and it was of great value in the cultivation of better turnips, thus enabling Aberdeenshire farmers to become famous as cattle-breeders. (The use of powdered bone as a fertilizer was introduced by the **Rev. Dr. Robertson of Ellon,** who was at one time headmaster of Robert Gordon's College in Aberdeen.)

It was during the nineteenth century that imported fertilizers, such as **Guano,** manure from the sea-birds which nest along the coast of Peru, and **Nitrate of Soda** from Chile were first used.

As well as using more fertilizers, farmers worked out good crop rotations, which improved the output without ruining the soil. A six year rotation became most popular. The biggest change in the crops grown was in the large increase in the amount of turnips and sown grasses. The old kind of barley, or bere, was replaced by a new variety and an earlier-ripening type of oats was cultivated in an effort to have the harvest finished before the winter frosts set in.

Aberdeen-Angus and Shorthorn Beef Cattle

Due to the improvement in feeding stuffs, which resulted from the increase in the use of fertilizers and better crop rotations, there was a big change in the cattle-breeding side of farming. **Aberdeen-Angus** cattle were developed in the north-east from the **Buchan Humlies** and other cattle known as **Angus Doddies,** while **Shorthorns** were imported from the south. Both breeds became very popular and quickly replaced the long-horned cattle, the last of which died in 1883 on the farm of Pitbee in Pitcaple. The introduction of these two breeds meant that instead of breeding lean cows for working and then driving to the trysts, farmers concentrated on rearing much fatter cattle, purely for beef.

William McCombie of Tillyfour did most to develop the Aberdeen-Angus breed in the County. His herd was so famous that Queen Victoria visited Tillyfour to see some of the cows, which had won nearly two hundred prizes at shows and exhibitions. Several farmers bought cows from McCombie and well-known Aberdeen-Angus herds, containing cattle bred at Tillyfour, were established at such places as Castle Fraser, Fyvie Castle, Conglass in the Garioch, Easter Skene, and Indego in Tarland.

The Shorthorn breed was introduced to Aberdeenshire in 1834 by **Alexander Hay of Shethin.** About four years later, the most famous of all the Shorthorn herds was started at **Sittyton** by **Anthony** and **Amos Cruickshank.** When the Sittyton herd was finally sold, many of the cows went to the **Bapton Manor** Shorthorn herd in England. (The Bapton Manor herd is now back in Aberdeenshire, at **Cairnbrogie** near Tarves.) Other Shorthorn herds were begun in the nineteenth century at Mains of Pitfour, Uppermill in Tarves, Kinellar, and **Collynie,** where **William Duthie's** herd soon became world-famous. (The **Duthie Experimental Stock Farm,** which is part of the **Rowett Research Institute,** was established in memory of William Duthie by his nephew.)

Sale of Livestock

The breeding of Aberdeen-Angus and Shorthorn cattle was made possible by the change which took place in the method of sending cows to market. Fat cattle, bred solely for beef, would not have been able to walk in droves to the trysts and still be in good condition. It was only when they could be moved to southern markets by ship, and later by rail, that the big developments in the breeding of cattle became possible and, at the same time, droving quickly died out.

The first weekly cattle-sale was held in Aberdeen in 1850 and others were soon established elsewhere in the County. As in the droving days, cattle were sold by private bargain. Then, in 1868, a cattle dealer named John Duncan began to sell his cows by auction in King Street, Aberdeen. This was the first Auction Mart in the area. Once railways had been laid in Aberdeenshire, (See Chapter 14) cows were transported in trucks, and marts were established in many places in the County. The amount of business which they did increased so rapidly that most of the local fairs died out. Some, such as Aikey Fair, Aulton Fair in Aberdeen, St. Lawrence Fair in Old Rayne, and Skippy Fair in New Deer kept going, but the time soon came when neither cows nor horses were sold at them.

Agricultural Clubs and Associations

To encourage farmers to undertake improvements, several agricultural clubs were formed. For example, the Formartine Agricultural Association, established in 1829, held its annual show of livestock at Udny Green; the Turriff Agricultural Association, established in 1830, held two shows yearly for the exhibition of animals and seeds; and the Vale of Alford Agricultural Association, established in 1831, held shows for cattle, seeds, and root crops such as turnips. These clubs were obviously trying to encourage the breeding of better livestock and the growing of better crops. Another, the **Garioch Farmer Club,** established in 1808, not only tried to encourage stock-breeding and the cultivation of turnips, ryegrass, and clover, but also attempted to improve the standard of ploughing by arranging ploughing-matches. It offered prizes to tenant-farmers who had done most in the reclaiming of land and the building of better steadings. It also offered a prize for an essay on the results of using different fertilizers and, as early as 1816, it sent a man to Edinburgh to train as a veterinary surgeon so that he could return to the Garioch and attend to sick animals. During the nineteenth century, therefore, the agricultural clubs attempted to make the farmers use new methods, new machines, and the latest discoveries of the scientists.

New and Better Leases for Tenant-farmers

Many of the improvements might not have been carried out, especially on the smaller farms where money and labour were scarce, if the system of leasing the land had not been altered. By the early years of the nineteenth century, three changes had taken place. Tenants were given longer leases, of nineteen years or more, and so were able to profit from any changes they made: before then, with short leases of five or seven years, it was not worth while for tenants to try to reclaim land or build good steadings for there was always the possibility that, by the time the improvements were completed, the lease would be finished, and they would be put off the land without benefiting from their hard work. Landlords promised to give compensation for improvements and if the tenant left the farm at the end of the lease he was repaid some of the money which he had spent on such things as enclosing and draining. Instead of paying rents mostly in goods and services (See chapter II) tenants now paid wholly in money and so could concentrate on their own farms.

At the end of the nineteenth century, farming was not in as good a state as we should expect from all the improvements which had been made. From 1878, more and more food was being imported and there was a time of poor prices. Many farmers found it difficult to make a good living and in the 1890's some of them left the crofts and smaller farms. Landowners were forced to combine several small farms and lease them to one tenant since few people wished to become tenant-farmers. Nevertheless, if somebody who had known Aberdeenshire in 1800 could have visited it in 1900 he would have found it hard to believe that such progress could have been made in a hundred years. With the reclaiming of land and the improvements in implements and fertilizers, with the greater attention to stock-breeding and the use of scientific discoveries, there had indeed been an agricultural revolution in Aberdeenshire, and other farmers could have been described in the same way as **Charles Murray** spoke of "Belcanny":

" Belcanny is foggin' wi' sillar laid by,
   Wi' byres fu' o' feeders and pedigree kye,
   Wi' horse in fine fettle for plough or for harrow,
   An' a' the tools needit fae binder to barrow.''

Chapter 14

THE INDUSTRIAL REVOLUTION

While improvements were being made in farming, great changes were also taking place in the other industries of Aberdeenshire. The gradual application of water power and then steam to the textile industry brought an end to the **Domestic System;** that is, the making of goods by hand in the workers' own homes, and led to the establishment of the **Factory System;** that is, the production of goods, usually by power-driven machines, in special buildings. Transport and communications were greatly improved. There was a big increase in trade by road, rail, and water, and thriving fishing, paper, and granite industries were established. The north-east, however, lost its position as the leading shipbuilding area in Scotland because of the concentration of the industry on Clydeside after the introduction of iron steam-ships.

Textiles

Woollen and worsted goods had been among the main Aberdeenshire exports since Stewart times. The manufacture of these goods was organised as a cottage industry, which reached its peak in the eighteenth century. In Rhynie, for example, the women, boys, and old men earned enough to pay the rent by knitting stockings, and in the Kincardine o' Neil area, about six hundred women were employed knitting stockings or spinning woollen thread at a weekly wage of about 2/6d. The spinning was done by "rock and spindle" and, from about the middle of the eighteenth century, on a spinning-wheel, driven by hand or by pedals, in the women's own kitchens. The thread was then woven into cloth on a hand-loom, usually by the men in the household. Spinning and weaving were carried on in addition to the normal everyday jobs of the workers. Clothiers, who paid accordingly to the amount produced and not by an hourly wage, often gave out wool to be spun, collected the yarn, and then gave it out to be woven. For example, the firm of **W. Spence & Son** was established in **Huntly** in 1780, but their spinning and weaving was done in the surrounding farms for several years after that.

The same system was followed in the stocking industry and some "shank merchants", as they were called, had as many as four hundred people working for them, all in their own homes. The merchants supplied the raw materials and then collected the finished articles, which they sold at prices ranging from 1/- to £5 5/- per pair to places as far afield as London, Hamburg, and Leningrad.

At first, little attention was paid to linen manufacture and only coarse cloth was made. In 1737, however, the **Duke of Gordon** invited **Hugh Macveagh** to come from Ireland to Huntly and supervise the manufacture of fine yarn. A few years later, Aberdeen spinners were instructed by a fully qualified woman and by the end of the century, more thread was made in the town than anywhere else in Scotland. Elsewhere in the County there was a rapid increase in the linen industry during the second half of the eighteenth century. New villages, such as Cuminestown, New Byth, Stuartfield, New Pitsligo, and Fetterangus, were established by landowners anxious to encourage linen manufacture.

Merchants distributed both imported and home-grown flax to be dressed, spun, and woven in the workers' own cottages. One, for example, had agents at Strathdon and Inverurie who handed out the flax, collected the finished product, and paid the workers, who usually earned about 6d. or 7d. a day, depending on their output.

Flax had to be carefully weeded and then, having been pulled by hand, set up to dry in sheaves. It was "rippled" to remove the seeds. The fibre was then separated from the stalk by steeping the flax in water for about ten days, spreading it out to dry on the grass, and then hanging it over a wooden board and beating, or "scutching", it with a wooden knife. The fibre was afterwards "heckled", or teased into strips, with a steel-toothed comb, spun on a spinning wheel, and woven on a hand-loom. The newly-made linen was a dirty grey colour and so it was bleached. This was a tedious business and often took as long as eight months. Sour milk and wood ashes were the bleaching agents and the cloth was washed in the bleachfields — special fields set aside for the purpose — with water baled from trenches by means of big wooden scoops. In 1785, however, a French scientist invented a method of bleaching by using chlorine, which was much quicker, and it was introduced to Aberdeen two years later.

Great advances were made in spinning and weaving in Aberdeenshire in the 1780's with the importation from England of **Hargreaves'** "spinning jenny" and **Kay's** "flying shuttle", but it was the introduction of power-driven machinery which brought about a revolution in the textile industry. Such machines could not be installed in cottages and, since it was no longer possible for workers to combine agriculture and manufacture, many people moved into the towns to seek employment in the newly-established mills.

In 1790, **Charles Baird,** an Aberdeen wool merchant, visited Rochdale and bought two carding machines. These, driven by water, were set up at Stoneywood and were used for combing out wool before it was spun. Within the next ten years, similar machines were introduced at Bucksburn, Fintray, Garlogie, Old Deer, Huntly, Strichen, and Turriff. At the beginning of the nineteenth century, a factory with twenty steam-driven machines for making woollen stockings, frocks, and mitts was erected in Aberdeen and the domestic woollen industry quickly died out when similar factories were erected within the next few years.

Water-driven scutching machines were introduced in the linen industry about 1730 and gradually the flax fibres came to be separated in lint mills instead of in the home. In 1790, a water-powered flax spinning mill was set up at **Grandholm** on the River

Don and it soon became the biggest linen mill in Scotland. Another mill, driven by steam, was established in Aberdeen in the early years of the nineteenth century, but by this time the industry was on the decline because of the cheapness of cotton.

Cotton spinning was begun in Aberdeenshire in 1785 when a mill was set up on the River Don on the outskirts of Aberdeen. The machines were driven by water and the workers are said to have been trained in Derbyshire at the factory belonging to **Richard Arkwright,** the inventor of the "water frame". About twenty years later, another cotton mill, in which the machinery was driven by two steam engines, was built in the suburbs of Aberdeen on the banks of the River Dee. Many children between the ages of nine and fifteen were employed in these mills, for long hours, and at little wages. This, together with the poor housing conditions of the mill-workers in the overcrowded towns, was one of the bad results of the industrial revolution.

The working conditions of the weavers were also very bad. They were employed in the factories for fourteen hours a day, at a weekly wage of from 3/6d. to 5/6d. Many of them worked the whole night through once per week to add to their meagre incomes. Although power-looms were in use at Grandholm in the early years of the nineteenth century, most other factories continued to rely mainly on hand-looms until the 1850's, when the Factory System completely displaced the Domestic System.

Roads

The development of the Factory System led to an increase in trade. Raw materials and manufactured goods had to be transported as quickly and as cheaply as possible and so it was necessary to improve the roads.

At the beginning of the eighteenth century, no attempt was made to construct good roads. The direction was roughly marked out, the larger stones were removed, and the deeper hollows filled in, but nothing was done to provide a permanent surface and the road soon became rutted, being usually covered in mud during the winter. It was impossible to go from Aberdeen to Monymusk in a horse-drawn carriage in 1720 and, in spite of attempts to improve the roads, a journey from Aberdeen to Finzean by horse-drawn chaise was still a remarkable feat in 1764. In 1770, it took two days to go from Aberdeen to Edinburgh by stage-coach and the passengers had to stay overnight at Perth.

An Act of Parliament was passed in 1719 stating that everyone had to help in repairing the roads for six days a year without payment, or give 1/6d. instead so that somebody else could be hired to do the work. Two years later, a General Surveyor of all roads and bridges in Aberdeenshire was appointed, but little improvement was made in road-making. From 1741, the practice of spreading small stones and shingle to form a surface was adopted, and in 1756 an act was passed ordering that all public highways in the County must be at least twenty feet wide and have ditches for drainage at each side. At the same time, farmers were told to stop ploughing across the roads! In the previous year, each parish had been made responsible for the upkeep of its own roads but, apart from two military highways, one built from Cairn o' Mount to Huntly by way of Potarch, Alford, and Clatt in 1746, and the other from Braemar northwards by Crathie, Gairnshiel, and Corgarff in 1754, the standard of road-making in Aberdeenshire continued to be very low until the last few years of the eighteenth century.

In 1795, the first **Turnpike Act** applying to Aberdeenshire was passed. (Turnpike Acts permitted the formation of local **Turnpike Trusts** with powers to build roads and to charge **Tolls** from all who used them.) Other Acts followed and, especially in the first quarter of the nineteenth century, many miles of good roads were constructed.

Turnpikes were much better than the old roads. They were about forty feet wide, with reasonably even surfaces. The middle part, fourteen feet wide, was made of granite chips covered with gravel, while the thirteen feet strip at either side of this "metalled" part was of smooth, tightly packed earth. The main turnpikes linked Aberdeen with Aboyne, Alford, Huntly, Turriff, Fraserburgh, and Peterhead. From about 1810, "water-bound macadamising" came into use. This method of providing hard surfaces on the roads, which could then be used by wheeled vehicles at all seasons of the year, was invented by **John Macadam.** (Tar was first used on the roads in 1907 to keep down the dust raised by motor traffic and was so successful that the process of "tarmacadamising" was generally adopted from then onwards.) The turnpike system lasted until 1865 when, by the **Aberdeenshire Road Act,** tolls were abolished and local authorities were empowered to collect rates for the upkeep of the roads in each of the eight districts into which the County was divided for this purpose.

The immediate effect of the opening of the turnpikes was an increase in the number of stage-coaches. In 1804, a two-wheeled, canvas-covered vehicle began to run between Aberdeen and Huntly. It carried four passengers inside and one outside with the driver. It was soon replaced by a bigger, four-wheeled carriage, which, carrying six inside passengers, had glass windows at the front and sides, a door at the back, and padded seats. There was no fixed time-table and the driver often made detours to pick up or set down passengers. The journey from Aberdeen to Huntly cost seven shillings and the average speed was about five miles an hour. Soon there were daily coach services linking Aberdeen with Inverness, Perth, Edinburgh, Peterhead and Kincardine o' Neil. There were also regular mail coaches and covered wagons for the transport of goods.

The Aberdeen-Port Elphinstone Canal

In spite of the improvement in road transport, it was still difficult to carry large quantities of goods in bulk for long distances. The Aberdeen to Port Elphinstone Canal was built to help to solve this problem. Surveyed by **Thomas Telford**, the famous Scottish civil engineer, it was between 18 and 19 miles long, 21 to 23 feet wide, and about 4 feet deep. It had seventeen locks and reached its highest point at Stoneywood. The first boats sailed on it in 1805, but it had to be closed for repair when many of the locks failed to work because of faulty masonry. The canal was officially opened in 1806, and by 1834 twelve boats were plying regularly between Port Elphinstone and Aberdeen harbour, where such cargoes as stones, slates, meal, oats, barley, lime, and coal could be transferred directly to or from the ocean-going ships.

The canal played a big part in the development of the Garioch as one of the foremost farming areas in the north-east, and was also used for passenger traffic. Two fly-boats, each pulled by two horses, made the return journey twice daily at a speed of about 8 m.p.h. When the Kittybrewster to Huntly railway was constructed in 1854, the canal went out of use and sections of the cutting were adapted for the railway track.

Railways

The first railway in Aberdeenshire was on Deeside, where the Aberdeen to Banchory section was opened in 1853, the Banchory to Aboyne section in 1859, and the Aboyne to Ballater section in 1866. It was originally intended to lay the Banchory to Aboyne line by way of Kincardine o' Neil but the laird objected that it would spoil his estate and so it went by Torphins and Lumphanan. A start was made with the Ballater to Braemar section but it was abandoned after reaching Foot of Gairn. Lack of money also led to plans for a railway from Culter to Alford, by way of Garlogie and the Loch of Skene, being dropped. A line to Coull and Tarland was surveyed but no work was done on it.

In the eleven years after the opening of the Kittybrewster to Huntly line, railways were laid linking Aberdeen to Oldmeldrum in 1856; to Turriff in 1857; to Kemnay, Monymusk, and Alford in 1859; to Ellon, Maud, and Mintlaw in 1861; to Peterhead in 1862; and to Fraserburgh in 1865. These lines all met at Guild Street in Aberdeen when the Joint Station was opened in 1867.

The engine-drivers on these early trains had no cabins and were protected by small windscreens. Wooden blocks, applied to the wheels of the tender and of the guard's van by hand levers, were the only means of braking the train and in order to ensure a gradual stop the steam was shut off long before the station was reached. The First Class carriages, which were modelled on the stage-coach, had a rail for luggage on top and an outside seat and foot-rail for the conductor. The seats were upholstered and the carriages were divided into compartments. The Third Class carriages had narrow, bare seats, small doors, windows which rattled loudly, and they were not divided into compartments. Each pasenger was allowed, by law, sixteen inches of seating. (This law has not been changed.) There were no restrictions on the number of coaches in a train, and passenger and goods traffic were mixed until the Board of Trade forbade it except on small branch lines, such as the one, opened in 1903, between Fraserburgh and St. Combs. The railways were invaluable to the districts through which they passed. New villages, such as Dinnet and Alford, were built along their routes; the timber trade benefited; new quarries were opened to supply granite chips; stores were erected for the distribution of manufactured and raw materials and for the collection of farm produce; and travel became increasingly more common.

The Clippers

Before the coming of the railways, the bulk of long-distance trade had been carried in locally-built sailing ships. Aberdeen and Peterhead were two of the leading shipbuilding centres in Scotland at the beginning of the nineteenth century, but the development of iron steamships led to their decline when the industry came to be concentrated on Clydeside.

Aberdeen, however, was able to hold its own for a time because of its famous clippers. Several of these long, slender, tall-masted, big-sailed vessels, with curved stems and sterns, were built between 1839 and 1869. They were designed for speed for the tea trade with China and the wool trade with Australia. The most famous Aberdeen-built clipper was the **Thermopylae** which defeated the **Cutty Sark** in one of the annual races from Shanghai to England. (The world-renowned "Cutty Sark" although built on Clydeside, was designed by a naval architect who was trained with A. Hall & Company in Aberdeen.)

The opening of the Suez Canal in 1869 and the improvement in boiler-making, which led to better steam engines, meant that the clippers could no longer compete with the steamships. Aberdeen shipbuilders therefore concentrated on small cargo and passenger steamers, tugs, and fishing vessels and, from about 1880, shipbuilding ceased in Peterhead apart from the construction of fishing boats.

Fishing

The introduction of steam power and improvements in shipbuilding resulted in great changes in the herring and white fishing industries. For a long time, the Dutch had a monopoly of the herring fishing in the North Sea, and even in 1800 few Aberdeenshire boats were engaged in it. They seldom went out of sight of land and fished with home-made hemp nets, which were much heavier than the cotton and nylon nets in use to-day.

Properly organised herring curing commenced at Fraserburgh about 1815, at Peterhead about 1820, and at Aberdeen about 1836. Boats from the small fishing villages, such as Boddam, St. Combs, Inverallochy, Cairnbulg, and Rosehearty caught fish for the curers in these towns. Each boat was under contract to supply so many crans, at a fixed price, to one curer, and any extra fish were usually bought at the curer's terms. This system lasted until sales by auction were introduced at the end of the nineteenth century. By that time, large fleets of well-built boats, based on Fraserburgh and Peterhead, were following the herring shoals as far afield as the Minch, the Shetland Islands, and East Anglia.

For most of the nineteenth century, Aberdeenshire fishermen used two sizes of boats. They were known locally as "sma' bates", or small boats, and "muckle bates", or big boats. The former were about twenty feet long, had five or six of a crew, and went to the white-fishing, while the latter were about forty-five feet long, had eight or nine of a crew, and engaged in herring fishing for a few weeks in the summer. These vessels were of the **Scaffie** or **Fifie** build. The former had curved bows and sloping sterns, and the latter had almost perpendicular bows and sterns. The boats had no decks and no cabins for their crews, who slept under the cover of a sail, and no navigation lights. If a crew suspected that there was another boat in the vicinity during the hours of darkness, they usually indicated their position by striking a flint. Cooking was done on an open fire on stones in the bottom of the boat. When not in use, the boats were drawn up on the foreshore above high-water level and so they had to be kept as light as possible. This, together with the lack of good harbours, the poverty of the fishermen, and the fact that undecked boats were considered essential for herring fishing, meant that the drifters continued to be restricted in size for most of the century.

In 1848, there was a big gale along the east coast and many boats were sunk, especially at Peterhead. As a result of a government inquiry which followed, fishermen were encouraged to build decked vessels. They were not willing to do so, however, and although the "Fishermen's Friend", the first decked fishing boat at Peterhead, was launched in 1858, it was another twenty years before most of the open boats had gone out of use. This change was due largely to the work of the **Royal National Lifeboat Institution** in building decked vessels and demonstrating their worth.

A new type of fishing vessel, the **Zulu,** appeared in 1879 when the "Nonesuch" was built at Lossiemouth. It had fifie bows and a scaffie stern, thus combining the good points of the two traditional designs. The scaffie quickly went out of use after this, but the fifie continued to be popular along with the zulu until displaced by steam drifters.

The first steam fishing vessel built in Scotland was launched in Aberdeen in 1871, but the sailing boats remained in use for many years after that. The first steam drifter in Fraserburgh, for example, was the "Faithlie", which began to fish in 1903. Even in 1910, almost half the total number of herring drifters from Aberdeen, Peterhead, and Fraserburgh were still driven by sail. Many of the early steamships, which, because of their long, thin funnels, were sometimes known as "pipe stalkies", also had sails and only used their engines as auxiliaries.

With the increased use of steam power, the herring industry was re-organised and working conditions became easier. The boats congregated at the larger harbours and many of the small fishing villages declined. Regular landings were possible since the vessels were no longer at the mercy of the winds and tides; larger catches were made as fishing was carried out at greater distances from the shore; and the fish could be quickly distributed to distant markets by means of railways. The nets, which were now machine-made of cotton, could be hauled with the help of the steam capstan, which could also be used to raise the masts and sails in the sailing vessels. The life of the fisherman's wife became easier. With the building of better harbours, she did not have to help to haul in and launch the boats. Nor did she have to carry her husband to his vessel so that he could proceed to sea dry-shod!

Probably the most revolutionary effect of the steam engine on fishing, however, was the development of trawling. It had been carried on, on a very limited scale, in the middle years of the nineteenth century by sailing trawlers keeping close to the land and never staying at sea for more than a day at a time. Trawling commenced in earnest in 1882 with a converted paddle-steamer, the "Toiler", which was purchased from Dublin where it had been a tug. In the following year, the first propellor-driven trawler to be built in Aberdeen, the "North Star", was launched from the yard of Duthie the shipbuilder at Footdee.

For most of the nineteenth century, fish were caught by means of the **Beam Trawl**, which was a triangular, flat, purse-shaped net, with the mouth extended by a wooden beam about fifty feet long. The net was dragged along for two or three hours on iron skids like sleigh runners, which kept it about three feet off the bed of the sea. In 1894, the **Otter Trawl** was introduced. As the net was pulled along it was now held open by two boards measuring about six feet by four feet. This type of trawl was more successful and was more easily handled than the "beam" trawl.

The earliest trawlers confined their activities to Aberdeen Bay and the grounds between Muchalls and Collieston, and landed their catches each day. Gradually, they moved north into the Moray Firth and beyond, much to the annoyance of the line fishermen, who attempted unsuccessfully to have trawling banned. The people of Fraserburgh even went as far as to stone any trawlermen who entered their harbour! Trawling continued to expand, however, and the Moray Firth was eventually closed to trawlers. Twenty-five years after the "Toiler" made its first trip, there were over two hundred steam trawlers based on Aberdeen and fishing many miles from their home port. They remained at sea for days on end and the fish which they caught were kept fresh in ice supplied from an ice factory, which was erected in Aberdeen in 1891.

In spite of the development of steam power, the whaling industry died out in Aberdeenshire. As early as 1757, there were three whalers in Aberdeen and in 1788 the first whaler from Peterhead went to Greenland. The industry flourished in these ports, and, to a lesser extent, in Fraserburgh during the first half of the nineteenth century, as many as thirty whalers going to Greenland from Peterhead alone in one year. From about 1860, the fleet rapidly declined and the last whaler left Peterhead in 1894. It was the "Windward", which became one of the vessels in an expedition to the North Pole and brought home the famous explorer, **Nansen** of the "Fram", in 1896. The well-known writer, **Conon-Doyle,** served as a doctor on a Peterhead whaler and based two books, "Gully of Bluemansdyke" and "Captain of the Pole Star", on his experiences.

Paper

An advertisement, which appeared on the 8th January, 1751, in the "Aberdeen Journal"— the north-east's first newspaper which had been established in 1748 — stated that **Bartholomew Smith,** a paper-maker from England, had erected a paper-mill on the Culter Burn. This, the oldest paper-mill in the north-east still in production, was set up in 1750 in a converted waulkmill, which had formerly been used for cleansing and shrinking home-spun woollen cloth.

The paper was made from linen rags, which Smith bought from the inhabitants of the surrounding district. Having been cut into strips and sorted into bundles according to colour, the rags were steeped in water, squeezed into balls, and allowed to ferment for six weeks. Then, by means of stamping-rods, which were shod with nails and driven by a water-wheel on the Culter Burn, the linen was shredded into small particles, while immersed in water. The pulp was poured into vats from which the paper-maker then filled his mould, shook it well so that the linen fibres were well intertwined, and the sheet of damp, spongy paper which was thus made was turned out on a felt of wool. A pile of sheets and felts was then pressed to squeeze out as much water as possible, after which the sheets were hung in a loft to dry on horse-hair ropes, which did not discolour the paper. To finish the process the sheets were passed through a tub of gelatine and sized so that they would not absorb ink.

A paper-mill was established at Stoneywood in 1770, one at Ferryhill in Aberdeen in 1803, and one at Mugiemoss in 1821. The Ferryhill mill did not prosper and its equipment was bought and transferred to the Culter mill in 1807. Four years later, there were fifty employees at Culter, working day-and-night shifts, and using new machines for making the paper. Stoneywood was equip-ped with these machines in 1822, by which time the Culter mills had gas lighting, and a stove and pipes for drying the paper, which were still made solely from rags. Indeed, as recently as 1879, rags were still the chief paper-making material. In 1860, how-ever, a mill was opened at Inverurie by **Thomas Tait & Son,** who pioneered the use of esparto grass in paper manufacture during the 1860's. The Aberdeenshire mills continued to expand and to-day many grades and varieties of paper are produced from rags, esparto grass, wood pulp, and mixtures of these, by the most modern equipment.

Granite

Aberdeenshire has long been famous for its granite. Quarrying first became profitable in the middle of the eighteenth century when Aberdeen granite began to be used for the pavements of London. In addition to the stones which were gathered off the land, stones were also collected from the sea-shore. The ever-increasing demand, however, led to the opening of several quarries from the end of the eighteenth century until, at the peak period of the industry, there were about thirty granite quarries in the County.

Among the most famous of these quarries were Kemnay and Peterhead, granite from which was used in the construction of the Forth and Tay Bridges, Tower Bridge and the Thames Embankment in London, Marischal College in Aberdeen, the Wallace Monument at Elderslie, and the harbours at Hull, Leith, Shields, Sunderland, and Newcastle, as well as the Bell Rock Lighthouse, which was built by Stevenson in 1808.

Granite came to be used extensively for statues and monuments. Hand-polishing of the stone was being carried on in Aberdeen in 1770 and at the same time, **Sir Archibald Grant of Monymusk** is said to have been experimenting with it. In 1832, **Alexander Macdonald** started polishing with a machine and in 1861 a granite-polishing works was established at Peterhead. From then on, the working of monumental granite became an increasingly important branch of the industry.

A big step forward was taken when steam power was applied to quarrying by **John Fyfe** at Kemnay. When he began operations in 1858, his tools were primitive and he had no machine for lifting heavy weights. By 1875, with the help of an inventor named **Andrew Barclay,** he had devised a steam derrick-crane, which was soon copied in other quarries, a steam hammer, and a "blondin". This was a cable-way, which, slung between two pylons, carried a "skip" for raising the quarried granite. It was named after Blondin, the famous acrobat, whom Fyfe had seen walking on a tight-rope across Golden Square in Aberdeen in 1861, and it has been copied all over the world.

The changes which took place in industry during the eighteenth and nineteenth centuries are known as the Industrial Revolution, but an even greater revolution was yet to come. Steam power had been largely the cause of the nineteenth-century changes, but, in the twentieth century, the internal combustion engine, and electrical and atomic power meant that the revolution was to continue at an ever-increasing rate.

THE ROLL OF HONOUR

Anderson, Sir Alexander (1802-1887) was born at Strichen, the son of a minister. He became a partner in the Aberdeen legal firm of Adam & Anderson, which promoted, in 1836, the North of Scotland Insurance Company (it is now the Northern Assurance Company) and the North of Scotland Bank. In 1838, he was largely responsible for the foundation of the Aberdeen Market Company, which built the Market in Market Street in 1842. He was also active in promoting the Great North of Scotland Railway and the Deeside Railway. From 1859 to 1866, he was Lord Provost of Aberdeen and during this time pushed forward the schemes for the building of the new Grammar School, finished in 1865, and the bringing of water from Cairnton near Banchory to Aberdeen. He was also very active in the discussions which led, in 1866, to sanction being given for the building of the new Municipal Buildings. He was knighted by Queen Victoria in 1863 when she was in Aberdeen to unveil the statue of the Prince Consort, which now stands in Union Terrace, Aberdeen.

Anderson, Sir George (1845-1923) born at Fraserburgh, was an accountant with the North of Scotland Bank in the Fraserburgh, Banff, Elgin, and Peterhead branches before being appointed Agent in the Huntly branch in 1873. He was promoted Agent in the Dundee branch in 1879, Assistant Manager in the Head Office in Aberdeen in 1888, and Manager in 1889. Owing to his successful re-organisation of the Bank's affairs, he was appointed to the Treasurership of the Bank of Scotland in 1898. He was knighted in 1905 by King Edward VII.

Barbour, John (c.1320-1396) was born probably at Aberdeen. He became minister at Old Rayne and Archdeacon of Aberdeen. In 1357, he was nominated by the Bishop of Aberdeen as one of the Commissioners who were to meet in Edinburgh to take measures for the liberation of King David, who had been a prisoner in England since the Battle of Neville's Cross in 1346. He wrote "The Brus", a vernacular poem dealing with the Wars of Independence. The oldest printed edition of this poem now known to exist was printed at Edinburgh in 1616.

Catto, Thomas Sivewright, First Baron Catto of Cairncatto (1879-1959) was born in Newcastle, where his father and mother, who were natives of Peterhead, lived for a short time. He was educated in the Old Peterhead Academy (now the Central School), and later at a college in Newcastle. He entered a shipping firm and became head of a company in India. During the First World War, he held various Government appointments and was created a Baronet in 1921. He retired from business in India in 1929 and became engaged in public affairs in London, being appointed a Director of the Bank of England, the Royal Bank of Scotland, and several companies connected with shipping and finance. He was elevated to the Peerage in 1936. During the Second World War, he again held several Government appointments, the most important of which was that of Financial Adviser to the Chancellor of the Exchequer. He became first Governor of the Bank of England in 1944 and held the post until 1949.

Chalmers, James (1713-1764) was born in Aberdeen, where he founded the "Aberdeen's Journal", the first newspaper north of the River Forth. First published in 1748, this paper is now known as "The Press and Journal" and is the oldest newspaper in Scotland.

Cheyne, George (1671-1743) was born at Methlick. Although at first intended for the ministry, he became a mathematician and a doctor. He published a book called "A New Theory of Fevers" before turning his attention to diet. At one time, he weighed 32 stones and was hardly able to walk but recovered largely because of a milk-and-vegetable diet. He published several books recommending temperance and vegetarianism and became widely known as a dietician.

Creighton, Dr. Charles (1847-1927), who was born at Peterhead, went to school there and at Old Aberdeen before graduating in Arts and Medicine in Aberdeen. He became the greatest British medical historian of the nineteenth century, his classic work being "The History of Epidemics in Britain".

Cruden, Alexander (1701-1770) was the son of an Aberdeen merchant and bailie. He wrote the "Complete Concordance to the Holy Scriptures", which became a classic. He began to call himself "Alexander the Corrector" and applied to Parliament to be appointed corrector of the national morals.

Dalgarno, George (1626-1687) was born in Old Aberdeen and became a teacher in Guernsey and Oxford, where he died. He proposed a universal language and laid the foundation for a universal shorthand. He was the author of "The Deaf and Dumb Man's Tutor" in which he expounded the hand alphabet.

Davidson, Thomas (1840-1900), born in a cottage at Toux in the parish of Old Deer, was a linguist and the author of works on medieval philosophy, education, and art.

Duncan, Dr. John (1796-1870), the son of humble parents, was born in Aberdeen. He was the first missionary of the Church of Scotland to the Jews of Budapest and made many converts. He became known as "Rabbi Duncan" and was appointed Professor of Oriental Languages in New College, Edinburgh.

Duncan, Sir Patrick (1870-1943) was born at the farm of Fortrie, King Edward, where he was a classmate of Sir Arthur Keith (q.v.). After attending Edinburgh and Oxford Universities, he joined the Inland Revenue Department of the Civil Service. In 1901, he went to the Transvaal, of which he became Lieutenant General in 1906. In 1936, he was invested with the Grand Cross of St. Michael and St. George, and was appointed Governor General of South Africa. He died at Government House, Pretoria.

Dyce, William (1806-1864), who was born near Kingswells, became famous as a painter. He was Professor of Fine Arts in King's College, London, and had a considerable share in the decoration of the Houses of Parliament.

Farquhar, John (1751-1826) was born at Bilbo, Crimond. He studied chemistry and eventually became one of the richest men of his day, making a fortune from the manufacture of gunpowder.

Farquharson, Joseph (1846-1935), the well-known painter of the Scottish countryside, was born at Finzean, which was the source of most of his artistic material and the inspiration of his work. He was especially interested in painting scenes of everyday country life and had a picture exhibited in the Royal Scottish Academy at the age of 13 years.

Ferguson, Patrick (1744-1780) was born at Pitfour and invented the breech-loading rifle during the American War of Independence. After demonstrating it, he was sent to America to form a corps of riflemen and was killed in action.

Ferrier, Sir David (1843-1928) was born in Aberdeen and became famous for his researches on the brain. In 1889, he was appointed Professor of Neuro-pathology at King's College, London, and was also consulting physician at King's College Hospital.

Forbes, John (1733-1808) was usually known as Ian Roy Forbes of Skellater. He became an officer in the Portuguese army, rising to the rank of General. He took part in the Peninsular campaign during the Napoleonic Wars and accompanied the Portuguese Royal Family when they fled to Brazil. He was appointed Governor of Rio de Janeiro, where a monument was erected over his tomb in the Cathedral.

Forsyth, Rev. Dr. Alexander J. (1768-1843) was the son of the minister at Belhelvie, where he succeeded his father in 1790. He established a Savings Bank, the first of its kind in the North-East and, when Jenner's method of vaccinating with cowpox as a protection against smallpox was announced, he showed how far he was ahead of his time by studying the subject and vaccinating his parishioners. In 1807, he took out a patent for the Percussion Lock for fire-arms which he had invented. Although the British Army refused to adopt his invention for nearly thirty years, he did not sell it to the French when offered a big sum of money for it. There is a Memorial Tablet to him in the Tower of London and a replica of it in King's College, Aberdeen.

Gerard, Alexander (1792-1839); **Gerard, James G.** (1795-1833); **Gerard, Patrick** (1794-1848). These brothers, natives of Aberdeen, where their father was a Professor, explored the Himalayas and, as a result, constructed a map of a route across the Hindu Koosh. The last-mentioned made important meteorological observations.

Gibbs, James (1674-1754) was born in Aberdeen. He studied architecture for ten years in Italy before returning to Britain to design, among other buildings, the Radcliffe Library at Oxford and the West Church of St. Nicholas in Aberdeen. He is acknowledged as ranking next to Sir Christopher Wren.

Gill, Sir David (1843-1914) was born in Aberdeen and began work as a watchmaker in his father's business. He was interested in astronomy and was given charge of a private observatory at Dunecht. In 1879, he was appointed astronomer-royal in the Cape of Good Hope, where he carried out his greatest work, a catalogue of the stars in the southern hemisphere. He was a pioneer in applying photography to astronomy and laid the foundations of a successful method of calculating the sun's distance from the earth. He supervised the Geodetic Survey of Natal and Cape Colony. He was one of the only seven British subjects to receive the Prussian Order, "Pour la Mérite".

Gordon, Sir Alexander (1786-1815) was the grandson of the 3rd Earl of Aberdeen and spent his early childhood at Castle of Gight. He obtained a commission in the Third Foot Guards (later called Scots Guards) and served with distinction in the Napoleonic Wars, especially in Portugal and Spain. He was appointed A.D.C. to the Duke of Wellington and was fatally wounded at Waterloo while warning his chief of the danger to which he was exposing himself.

Gordon, George (1638-1729) was a Professor in Marischal College before he was thirty years old. He became President of the Court of Session and in 1680 was made a Lord of Session with the title of Lord Haddo. In 1682, he was appointed Lord Chancellor of Scotland and was created the first Earl of Aberdeen. He was buried in Methlick churchyard.

Gordon, George (1784-1860) was 3rd Earl of Aberdeen. After a brilliant career at Harrow and Cambridge, he entered the Foreign Office. He was British Ambassador in Vienna when only 29 years old. He was Foreign Secretary from 1828 to 1830 and again in 1841 to 1846. In 1852, he became Prime Minister but resigned in 1855.

Gordon, John Campbell (1847-1934) was 7th Earl of Aberdeen. He was High Commissioner to the General Assembly from 1881 to 1885, and in 1915. He was Viceroy of Ireland in 1886 and from 1906 to 1915; Governor General of Canada from 1893 to 1898; and Lord Lieutenant of Aberdeenshire from 1880 to 1934.

Gordon, Patrick (1635-1699) was born at Auchleuchries in the parish of Cruden and became a soldier of fortune in the service of Sweden, then Poland, and finally Russia, where he rose to the highest rank. His services to Russia were so valuable that Peter the Great is said to have wept at his death-bed.

Gordon, Robert (c. 1665-1732), born at Aberdeen, made his fortune as a merchant in Danzig and returned to Aberdeen, where he had a reputation of being a miser. In December, 1729, he executed and signed a deed of mortification disposing of his whole fortune, amounting to £10,000, for the founding and endowing of a hospital for the "maintenance, aliment, entertainment, and education of young boys whose parents are poor and indigent, and not able to maintain them at schools and put them to trades and employments". The original "Hospital", now known as Robert Gordon's College, was completed in 1739 and, after being occupied by the Duke of Cumberland's troops in 1746, was opened in 1750 with 30 boys.

Gregory, James (1638-1675) was the son of the minister at Drumoak. He was the most brilliant of the Gregory family, which, over a period of two hundred years, supplied fourteen professors to British Universities. He invented the reflecting telescope and, as a mathematical genius, has been placed second only to Newton, with whom he corresponded.

Gregory, James (1753-1821) was the great-grandson of the James Gregory mentioned above. He became Professor of the Practice of Medicine in Edinburgh. He became, as his father had been, First Physician to the King in Scotland. His name became a household word in connection with Gregory's Mixture.

Gregory, William (1803-1858) became Mediciner in King's College, Aberdeen in 1839, the fourth of the Gregory family to occupy the office. In 1844, he became Professor of Chemistry in Edinburgh, and was considered one of the most distinguished chemists of his time. He did much to popularise the theories of Liebig.

Guild, Dr. William (1586-1657) was a native of Aberdeen who was minister at King Edward from 1608 to 1631. He became one of the "Aberdeen Doctors" and Principal of King's College from 1640 to 1651, when he was deposed by Genral Monk. He was a great benefactor to the University and the City, especially the Incorporated Trades to whom he gifted the old Trinity Monastery and Chapel for use as a meeting-place. It was used as such until 1844, when the old buildings were demolished to make way for the construction of Exchange Street and Guild Street (named after the benefactor).

Henderson, David B. (1840-1906) was born in Old Deer, but emigrated to the U.S.A. with his parents. There he fought in the Union Army during the Civil War and then qualified as a lawyer. He was elected to the House of Representatives in 1883 and remained a member for the next twenty years. He was Speaker of the House from 1899 to 1903.

Hunter, Dr. William A. (1844-1898) was born in Aberdeen and had a brilliant career as a law student. He became a Professor in University College, London, and was elected M.P. for North Aberdeen. He played a large part in introducing entirely free elementary education in Scotland and was the first in Parliament to suggest Old Age Pensions.

Jamesone, George (1587-1644) was born in Aberdeen. He was a pupil of Rubens and a fellow-student of Vandyck. Probably the greatest of Scottish portrait painters, he came to be known as

111

"the Scottish Vandyck". He painted the portraits known as the "Sybils" for King's College, Aberdeen, as well as the portraits of many famous men, including Charles I.

Johnstone, Dr. Arthur (1587-1641) was born at Caskieben (later Keith Hall), which was the family estate. He received his early education at Kintore and visited Italy, Germany, Denmark, Holland, France, and England. He became famous as a writer of Latin verse, including a complete version of the Psalms.

Keith, Sir Arthur (1866-1955), world-famous scientist and anthropologist, was born at Quarry Farm at Persley near Aberdeen. He went to Woodside School, Aberdeen, until the family moved to Kinnermit Farm near Turriff. He subsequently attended school at Ardmiddle, Turriff, King Edward, and Robert Gordon's College, Aberdeen, before going to Aberdeen University. In 1899, he became secretary of the Anatomical Society of Great Britain, and was President of the Royal Anthropological Institute from 1912 to 1914. He was Conservator of the museum and Hunterian Professor at the Royal College of Surgeons, and lectured and wrote on the results of anthropological discoveries.

Keith, James Francis Edward (1696-1758), the youngest brother of the last Earl Marischal, was born at Inverugie Castle near Peterhead. After taking part in the Jacobite Risings of 1715 and 1719, he became a soldier-of-fortune. He served in Spain for nine years and in Russia, where he became Governor of the Ukraine, for nineteen years before entering the service of Frederick the Great of Prussia. By common consent the most distinguished soldier the North-East has produced, he displayed his outstanding ability during the Seven Years' War and was promoted Field Marshal. He was killed at Hochkirch in 1758. In 1868, William I of Prussia presented a statue of him — the replica of one in Berlin — to Peterhead.

Lamont, John (1805-1879) was born at Corriemulzie near Braemar. In later life, he assumed the name of Johann von Lamont. After studying at Ratisbon, Bavaria with the intention of becoming a Roman Catholic priest, he decided to make science his career and became Astronomer Royal of Bavaria in 1835. A monument to him was erected at Inverey by the Deeside Field Club.

Leslie, Alexander (1580-1661), a member of the Balquhain family, became a Field Marshal in the Swedish army under Gustavus Adolphus. He returned to Scotland and supported the Covenanters. He directed the military preparations in 1638, led the army in the Second Bishops' War, and was present at Marston Moor in 1644. He fought for the Royalists at Dunbar in 1650, and was a prisoner of the English Parliament from 1651 to 1654.

Leslie, Walter (1606-1667) was the son of John Leslie of Balquhain. He was a soldier-of-fortune in the service of the Emperor and fought with distinction in several battles. He saved Vienna from von Wallenstein, who was plotting against the Emperor, and had him slain. He became a Count and was promoted to Field Marshal.

Leslie, William (1657-1727), son of the 5th Laird of Warthill, was a graduate of Aberdeen University and, for a few years, headmaster of Chapel of Garioch School. He became a Roman Catholic and went to Rome in 1684. When he was 33 years old, he became Professor of Theology in the College of Padua. He subsequently became Bishop of Laybach, Metropolitan of Carniola, and a Prince of the Holy Roman Empire.

Liddel, Dr. Duncan (1561-1613) was born in Aberdeen and studied medicine and mathematics at King's College, Aberdeen, and on the Continent. He became Rector of Julian University and first physician to the Court of Brunswick. His books on medicine were known throughout Europe. He bequeathed Pitmedden estate for the benefit of six poor scholars and endowed a Chair in Medicine in Marischal College, Aberdeen. A granite obelisk, erected in his memory, stands in a field between Pitmedden Station near Dyce and the River Don.

Macaulay, Robertson (1833-1915) was born in Fraserburgh, but his family moved to Stornoway when he was 10 years old. After serving his apprenticeship as a solicitor in Stornoway and Aberdeen, he emigrated in 1854 to Canada, where he worked with insurance companies. In 1874, he was appointed secretary to the Sun Life Assurance Company of Canada, which was then a small undertaking. When the company expanded, he became successively manager, managing director, and then president and managing director. Under his direction, the Sun Life Company became the biggest insurance company in Canada and opened branches all over the world. He was succeeded as President of the company by his son, **Thomas Basset Macaulay** (1860-1942), the founder of the Macaulay Institute for Soil Research at Craigiebuckler, Aberdeen, and the Stornoway experimental farm for the utilisation of peat-land.

MacDonald, Dr. George (1824-1905) was born in Huntly and was educated there, at Aberdeen (Old) Grammar School, and Aberdeen University. After graduating, he became a minister in the Congregational Church but resigned after two years and devoted himself to lecturing and writing. He enjoyed a great reputation as a novelist and a poet, and numbered Ruskin, Lewis Caroll, and Lord Tennyson among his friends. Over a period of 42 years, he produced 52 volumes, including 25 novels, many of which had the scenes of his boyhood as background.

MacGillivray, James Pittendreigh (1856-1938) was born in Port Elphinstone, where there is a plaque on the front of the house in which he was born. He was a sculptor who exhibited in the Royal Scottish Academy at 16 years of age. He directed his efforts to the furtherance of Art education and to the promotion of interest in sculpture. The re-organisation of the Edinburgh College of Art was largely due to his efforts. His greatest works belong to the period 1895 to 1917, when he ranked as an international figure in sculpture. Outstanding among his works are the Burns Statue at Irvine, the John Knox Memorial in Edinburgh, and the National Memorial to Gladstone. He was appointed Sculptor in Ordinary to H.M. George V in 1921. He also published two books of poems, "Pro Patria" in 1915 and "Bog Myrtle and Peat Reek" in 1923.

MacGillivray, William (1796-1852) was born in Old Aberdeen and became Professor of Natural History in Marischal College in 1841. He was an ornithologist who became famous throughout Europe. His book, "Natural History of Deeside and Braemar", became a classic.

Macgrigor, Sir James (1771-1858) was the son of an Aberdeen merchant. In 1798, he was a leader of the students at Marischal College who founded a medical society which, in 1811, became the Medico-Chirurgical Society of Aberdeen. He became chief of the Medical Staff in the Peninsular campaigns during the Napoleonic Wars and was a pioneer of the humanitarian treatment of the sick and wounded in war. A granite obelisk was erected to his memory in the quadrangle at Marischal College, but was moved to the Duthie Park, Aberdeen.

Mackay, Alexander Murdoch (1849-1890) was born in the Manse at Rhynie, where he was taught by his father until he was 14 years of age when he entered Aberdeen Grammar School. He trained as a teacher in the Free Church Training College in Edinburgh and then studied mechanics and engineering at Edinburgh University. He worked as a volunteer teacher and then as a draughtsman with a firm near Berlin. As a result of reading Stanley's "How I Found Livingstone", he offered his services to the Church Missionary Society and was sent as a lay missionary and mechanic to Uganda. For the next fourteen years, he was largely responsible for the opening up of the country and the conversion of its people to Christianity.

McRobert, Sir Alexander (1854-1922) was the eldest son of John McRobert, Douneside, Tarland. He spent his early life in Stoneywood and then went as a clerk to Cawnpore Woollen Mills Company, India. He rose to be President of the Chamber of Commerce at Cawnpore. The McRobert Memorial Hall at Robert Gordon's College, Aberdeen, is a memorial to him.

Maitland, Dr. Charles (1668-1748) was a native of Methlick and is thought to be the first British doctor to inoculate against smallpox. His method of inoculating the patient with a slight attack of smallpox was later displaced by the safer and more successful method of vaccination with cowpox, which was discovered by Jenner. Maitland's first patient, in 1717, was the four-year old son of the British ambassador in Constantinople. After returning to Britain, Maitland continued his experiments and six prisoners who had been sentenced to death in Newgate Prison, London, in 1721, were set at liberty on condition that they allowed themselves to be inoculated by him to test the method. This was successful and he published a book entitled "Mr. Maitland's Account of Inoculating the Smallpox" which aroused much controversy. In spite of this, he was sent to Hanover in 1724 to inoculate the future Prince of Wales and was paid £1000 for doing so.

Manson, Sir Patrick (1845-1922) was born in Oldmeldrum and became head of the London School of Tropical Medicine. It was largely due to his researches that Sir Ronald Ross made the advances which led to the discovery that the mosquito spread malaria.

Mitchell, Charles (1820-1895), who was born in Aberdeen, became a shipbuilder on the Tyne. He transformed the wooden shipbuilding yard at St. Petersburg (Leningrad) into an iron shipbuilding yard. He was a great benefactor to Aberdeen University and the Mitchell Hall and Tower at Marischal College are named after him.

Murray, Charles (1864-1941), "Hamewith" the poet, was a native of Alford but spent most of his life in Africa. He was acknowledged as the best Scots poet of his day, and did much to prepare the way for the Scottish Literary Renaissance. His poems were published in three books: "Hamewith", "In The Country Places", and "The Sough o' War", which written mostly in the Scots dialect, contain such well-known poems as "The Whistle" and "It Wasna' His Wyte". He is buried in the old churchyard at Kirkton of Alford, where a Park is dedicated to his memory.

Ogilvie-Forbes, Sir George (1892-1954) of Boyndlie House, Tyrie, entered the Diplomatic Service after serving in the Middle East during the First World War. He held appointments in various countries including Sweden, the Vatican, Iraq, Spain, and Germany, before being appointed Ambassador to Cuba and then to Venezuela. He was made a Knight Commander of the Order of St. Michael and St. George before retiring.

Ogston, Sir Alexander (1844-1929) achieved world-wide fame as a pioneer in surgery and anaesthesia. In 1881, he discovered the pus organism. In the early years of the twentieth century, he was Professor of Surgery in Aberdeen University. He was also an enthusiastic archaeologist and the results of his investigations were published in a volume entitled "The Prehistoric Antiquities of the Howe of Cromar".

Ogston, Dr. Francis (1803-1887) was born in Aberdeen, the son of Alexander Ogston, the founder of a soap factory. He was Professor of Medical Jurisprudence in Aberdeen from 1857 to 1883. His text-book on the subject became the standard work in Europe.

Philip, John (1817-1867) was born in Aberdeen, where he began work as a house painter. He later studied in London and Spain and became one of the most famous artists in Scotland. Besides many portraits, he painted such famous pictures as "Presbyterian Catechising" and "Collection of the Offerings in a Scottish Kirk", the Kirk being the one which now stands in ruins at Belhelvie.

He also painted the scene when Queen Victoria presented the Colours which are still carried by the Lonach Highlanders at their annual Gathering at Bellabeg, Strathdon.

Ramsay, James (1733-1789) was born in Fraserburgh and studied medicine in King's College, Aberdeen, before becoming a surgeon in the navy. An accident at sea rendered him unable to continue his duties as a surgeon and he studied for the ministry of the Church of England. He was sent to St. Kitt's in the West Indies, where he acted not only as Rector but also as medical adviser to several plantations. He was the first person to write publicly against the slave trade in such pamphlets as "Essay on the Treatment and Conversion of African Slaves in the British Sugar Colonies".

Reid, Thomas (1710-1796) was a native of Strachan. He was minister at Newmachar, Professor in King's College, Aberdeen, and then Professor in Glasgow University. He became a well-known philosopher and created the "Scottish School" in opposition to David Hume, whose sceptical philosophy denied the existence of God and could see no connecting principle or purpose in life.

Robertson, Archibald (1765-1835) was born at Monymusk. After attending Aberdeen University, he studied art in Edinburgh and London. He was a favourite pupil of Sir Joshua Reynolds and became known as the "Reynolds of Scotland". He went to America and was one of the most notable pioneers of American Art.

Robertson, Joseph (1810-1866) was born in Aberdeen and was educated there and at Udny. He became Historical Curator of the Records in Edinburgh. Along with his friend and fellow-historian, John Hill Burton, he founded the Spalding Club to further historical research. Among his books are "A New Deeside Guide" and "The Book of Bon-Accord".

Ross, John (1699-1784) was a Deeside man who became schoolmaster at Lochlee. He was the author of "Helenore, or the Fortunate Shepherdess", a long pastoral poem in the Scots dialect, as well as of other poems and songs including "The Rock and The Wee Pickle Tow" and "To the Begging We Will Go".

Skinner, John (1721-1807) was for a long time minister at Longside and Dean of the Diocese of Aberdeen but his chief claim to fame is as a poet in the Scots vernacular. Among his most famous compositions are "The Ewie wi' the Crookit Horn", "The Monymusk Christmas Ba'in'", and "Tullochgorum", which Robert Burns pronounced the best Scots song ever written.

Slessor, Mary (1848-1915) was born in Aberdeen. Her father was a Buchan shoemaker and her mother came from Oldmeldrum. She worked at the age of 11 as a "half-timer" in a textile factory in Dundee. She volunteered to go as a missionary to Africa and arrived in Calabar in 1876. She lived in native huts in the jungle, where she fought witchcraft and disease, and earned the love and respect of the natives. After labouring for 39 years in Nigeria, she died and was buried there.

Smith, Rev. Robertson (1846-1894) was born in the former South Church Manse at Keig. He became Professor of Hebrew at Cambridge and was editor of the ninth edition of the Encyclopaedia Britannica.

Steell, Sir John (1804-1891) was the son of an Aberdeen woodcarver. He became a noted sculptor. Among his most famous works are the seated figure of Sir Walter Scott in the Scott Monument in Edinburgh — the first marble statue commissioned in Scotland; the memorial to the Black Watch in Dunkeld Cathedral; the statue of the Duke of Wellington in the Register House, Edinburgh; and the memorial to the Prince Consort in Charlotte Square, Edinburgh.

Thom, William (1798-1848), although born in Aberdeen, came to be known as the "Inverurie Poet". He worked as a weaver in Aberdeen but was forced to become a vagrant. After his wanderings, he settled in Inverurie, where his wife died and was buried in a nameless grave near the Bass. He himself died penniless in Dundee. Among the poems in his "Rhymes and Recollections of a Handloom Weaver" are "The Blind Boy's Pranks", "The Mitherless Bairn", and "The Wedded Waters".

Urquhart, John (1547-1631) was the builder of Craigston Castle. He was one of the most learned men of his day and was known as the "Tutor of Cromarty". He acted first as tutor, or guardian, to his grand-nephew, who was the chief of the Clan Urquhart, and then to his great-grand-nephew, the famous Sir Thomas Urquhart (q.v.).

Urquhart, Sir Thomas (1611-1660), who was born at King Edward, proposed a universal language. He also translated the works of Rabelais. He is said to have died in a fit of laughter when he heard that Charles II had been summoned back to the British throne.

Wood, Alexander (1871-1937) was born at King Edward and received his early education at Crudie School. He entered mission work in 1898 at Chanda in India. In 1926, he became Bishop of the huge diocese of Nagpur.

Wylie, Sir James (1768-1854), a graduate of King's College, Aberdeen, became head of the Russian Medical Department and is said to have performed two hundred operations on the field at the Battle of Borodino in 1812. He was medical adviser to several of the Czars and accompanied Alexander I to London, where he was created a baronet by the Prince Regent.

Printed by MIDDLETONS ABERDEEN LIMITED
Abbotswell Road Works, Aberdeen